PRAISE FOR
ANTHONY ROBLES

"*Unstoppable* is an inspirational narrative that captures the essence of conquering fears, breaking down barriers, and never letting one's dreams be shattered. This is truly the American spirit."
—Condoleezza Rice

"A living example of determination . . . simply remarkable."
—Ellen DeGeneres

"I am inspired by his courage. . . . [Anthony] is a reminder of the amazing things that can happen when we don't give in; when we hang on for just a little longer than our bodies and minds are telling us to."   —Jay Leno, from the Foreword

"*Unstoppable* is a really touching and absorbing account of Anthony's journey. I've really enjoyed the way he's taken me there to share it with him. This is a great book!"
—Serena Williams

"Anthony Robles beat the odds by becoming unstoppable on the mat and in life. He's an inspiration."
—Michael Oher, author of the
New York Times bestseller *I Beat the Odds*

"*Unstoppable* is filled with passion, empowerment, hope, and encouragement. Anyone who reads this book will walk away with a sense of self-motivation to go out and accomplish their dreams."

—LaDainian Tomlinson,
former NFL running back and Most Valuable Player

"Today's world is in need of heroes. After meeting Anthony and reading his book, I'm moved by his ability to inspire others to greatness—to be unstoppable. Anthony exemplifies greatness and reminds us that greatness lies in all of us."

—Elliott Hill, vice president of Nike North America

• • •

Anthony Robles is a three-time all-American wrestler and motivational speaker. A graduate of Arizona State University, he was the 2011 NCAA National Wrestling Champion. Also in 2011, Robles received ESPY's Jimmy V Perseverance Award as well as the NFL Hispanic Heritage Leadership Award. He was inducted into the National Wrestling Hall of Fame in 2012. He lives in Phoenix, Arizona.

Austin Murphy is a senior writer at *Sports Illustrated*. He is the author of *The Sweet Season* and four other books.

UNSTOPPABLE

FROM UNDERDOG TO UNDEFEATED:
HOW I BECAME A CHAMPION

ANTHONY ROBLES

with Austin Murphy

BE UNSTOPPABLE!

Anthony Robles

GOTHAM BOOKS

**To my family and friends who helped me along
my journey, and to the sport of wrestling**

GOTHAM BOOKS
Published by the Penguin Group
Penguin Group (USA) Inc., 375 Hudson Street,
New York, New York 10014, USA

USA | Canada | UK | Ireland | Australia
New Zealand | India | South Africa | China

Penguin Books Ltd, Registered Offices: 80 Strand, London WC2R 0RL, England
For more information about the Penguin Group visit penguin.com.

Published by Gotham Books, a member of Penguin Group (USA) Inc.
Previously published as a Gotham Books hardcover

First trade paperback printing, September 2013
10 9 8 7 6 5 4 3 2 1

Gotham Books and the skyscraper logo are trademarks of Penguin Group (USA) Inc.

The Library of Congress has catalogued the hardcover edition as follows:

Robles, Anthony, 1988–
Unstoppable : from underdog to undefeated : how I became a champion / Anthony
Robles.
p. cm.
ISBN 978-1-592-40777-4 (hardback) 978-1-592-40804-7 (paperback)
1. Robles, Anthony, 1988–   2. Wrestlers—United States—Biography.
3. Athletes with disabilities—United States—Biography.   I. Title.
GV1196.R63A3 2012
796.812092—dc23
[B] 2012021191

Printed in the United States of America
Set in Janson Text
Designed by Spring Hoteling

While the author has made every effort to provide accurate telephone numbers and
Internet addresses at the time of publication, neither the publisher nor the author as-
sumes any responsibility for errors, or for changes that occur after publication. Further,
the publisher does not have any control over and does not assume any responsibility for
author or third-party Web sites or their content.

Penguin is committed to publishing works of quality and integrity.
In that spirit, we are proud to offer this book to our readers;
however, the story, the experiences, and the words
are the author's alone.

CONTENTS

FOREWORD

by Jay Leno

I met Anthony Robles on July 14, 2011, just before presenting him with the Jimmy V Award for Perseverance at the ESPYs in Los Angeles. We were standing in the wings, just off camera. Anthony told me he was a bundle of nerves, but I wasn't buying it. Moments later, I handed him his trophy, then watched him knock his acceptance speech out of the park.

I left the theater that night thinking two things: (1) I need to redefine what I think of as "hardship"; and (2) get this kid on the show.

Not quite a week later, we did. Walking onto the stage at *The Tonight Show* looks easy enough. But the experience has intimidated more than a few seasoned Hollywood veterans. The lights are bright, the audience is live, and the program is broadcast to millions of people all over the world. But Anthony walked out, flashed that thousand-watt smile, pulled up a chair, and told his story like he was sitting in his own living room. He was humble and genuine, and he made an instant connection with the audience.

We talked first about his mother, who is no less extraordinary than her son the NCAA champion. Judy Robles conceived Anthony when she was sixteen, yet never considered giving him up for adoption, even when he was born with one leg. She was just a kid herself, really, yet it was up to her to strike the right balance between sheltering her son—a mom's first instinct—and exposing him to the taunts and stares that were bound to follow him. She knew that kids can be mean, and that her boy was going to have a rough go. She also knew it would then be up to her to assure him, every day, that just because he was different, there was nothing he couldn't do.

It would've been a daunting challenge for anyone, let alone a teenage mother. But Judy was up for the challenge. To meet Anthony is to see that she nailed it.

"My mom raised me with my head in the clouds," he told me on the show that night. "She raised me to believe I could do anything I wanted. And really, I thought I was Superman."

The truth is, I'm not sure Superman could do one hundred pull-ups in two minutes, or bench 320. The Caped Crusader would've killed for Anthony's physique. Have you seen this kid's arms? He makes Michelangelo's *David* look like Peter in *Family Guy*.

After struggling in his first season as a wrestler, Anthony learned to drop down onto the mat, forcing his opponents to attack his strength: that jacked upper body. In the beginning, when he was still figuring out his style—when his mother considered it a victory if her spindly boy didn't get pinned—people pitied him: *He's only got one leg—it's not fair!*

Later, when he learned to play to his strengths and camouflage his weaknesses, when he started pinning opponents left and right, some came to see his missing leg in a different light. It gave him an advantage! It allowed him to carry more muscle on his upper body! It gave opponents one fewer limb to grab hold of! *He's only got one leg—it's not fair!*

While such ignorance annoys me, it makes Anthony smile. "When they're hating on you," he told me, "it means you must be doing something right."

No matter how much he struggled on the mat, the wrestling room was a refuge for him, a place he could go to escape the trials of his home life. Those challenges were far more painful and difficult than anything he faced as a wrestler and, to my mind, make up the most poignant and interesting parts of this book.

Like everyone who knows Anthony's story, I'm inspired by his courage. I also appreciate his honesty. It was interesting to find out that on several occasions, he almost walked away from the sport he loved. When his stepdad would disappear for weeks at a time, leaving his mom and four siblings wondering how they were going to eat, Anthony came *this* close to quitting in order to get a job to help pay the bills.

That he didn't quit, that he came back for one final season in the sport "God put him on this earth to do," as Judy puts it, is a reminder of the amazing things that can happen when we don't give in; when we hang on for just a little longer than our bodies and minds are telling us to.

After I handed him that silver ESPY, but before he entranced the audience by reciting the poem that sums up who he is (and helps explain the title of this book), Anthony spoke these promising words:

"And now, as I go forward with so much more to do . . ."

I, for one, am very much looking forward to seeing what Anthony can accomplish in his life after wrestling. I have no idea where, or how, he'll make his mark: whether it's as a motivational speaker, a TV analyst, or back in the ring, giving Mixed Martial Arts a shot. (Judy's down on that idea, but Anthony refuses to rule it out. Pity the fool that takes him lightly.) All I know is that I'm not going to make the mistake of underestimating him, of telling him there's something he can't do.

The guy thinks he's Superman. Look at what he's done already. Who are we to argue?

INTRODUCTION

Mother Knows Best

***THERE** is nothing wrong with you.* That was the message I got throughout my childhood from my mom, Judy Robles, who bore me at the age of sixteen, and who told me over and over, no matter what I'd heard in school that day, that I was complete, that I was perfect. Because I was young and trusting, I believed her. And so, in perfect seriousness, at the age of seven, I set a goal for myself to someday play for the Oakland Raiders.

By the time I was fourteen, hopping around as a ninety-pound defensive tackle on the freshman team, I realized that wasn't going to happen. You've probably heard the saying about how when the Lord closes a door, somewhere He opens a window. The year I quit football was the year I took up wrestling. That trade has worked out okay for me. While I never did play a down for the Raiders, I was invited to deliver a speech to the team on the eve of a game in November 2011. I'm a guy with a Raiders shield tattooed on my left deltoid. So, yes, it was a kick, sharing my message with the players and coaches, visiting the Black Hole for the first time in my life, then getting a standing ovation when I was recognized at midfield during the game.

Making the experience even sweeter was that, after learning my entire family is nuts for the Silver and Black (my mom also sports a Raiders tat), the team flew her and my four siblings to Oakland for that game. We were greeted at the airport, then driven to Raiders headquarters, where we met the players and coaches, then had dinner with the team. I gave a motivational talk to the team; it went really well. While I was on the sideline for the next day's game, my mom was up in one of the suites, chatting up Silver and Black Hall of Famers Willie Brown and Fred Biletnikoff. It was a dream come true for all of us. It made me truly happy to be able to share these experiences with my family and give back to them for their unconditional love.

You see, even though I was born with one leg, my mom never allowed me to use that as an excuse to hold back, to sit on the sidelines, to miss out on life. I grew up doing all of the same things that other kids did. I rode a bike, took jiujitsu lessons, and raked leaves with my brother for money. I played baseball, basketball, and football (safety in seventh and eighth grade; defensive tackle in ninth). And on the night my friends and I made some dry-ice bombs that happened to go off in the park just as a squad car was rolling by, I ran from the cops, right alongside my two-legged buddies.

When I say that I "ran," I mean I crutched as fast as I could. Which, if I do say so myself, can be pretty fast. The first time my wrestling coach at Arizona State timed us in the mile, I finished in ten minutes. I eventually got that down to eight. The first time he sent the team out on one of our preseason 6 A.M. six-milers, head coach Shawn Charles gave me an out: "Anthony, you don't have to do this." But I explained to him that I do everything everyone else on the team does.

That explains my conflicted reaction to being nominated for the Best Male Athlete with a Disability ESPY Award after winning the national championship in my weight class in high school: I was flattered by the nomination but angered by the name of the category. I don't see myself as disabled. What am I unable to do? (You know, other than dance. And maybe play kickball at an elite level.)

When you lose a wrestling match—and I lost a lot, early on—you have no one but yourself to blame. That sense of self-reliance and accountability are what initially attracted me to the sport in junior high. My cousin Jesse, who's now a police officer in San Diego, wrestled at Salpointe High in Tucson. He's the one who first talked me into pulling on the headgear and venturing out onto the mat. When he was first selling me on it, he made this point: "The football players are the big guys at high school, but we're the *tough* guys," he said. "They don't like to take us on because they know we can take them down."

I liked that part of it, too.

AT a time when my own house didn't feel like home, when the situation with my stepdad was at its most tense—when he paced around in a cold fury or engaged in shouting matches (and worse) with my mom—wrestling became my refuge. It opened many doors for me—to Arizona State University, to national championships, and to that night in July 2011 at the Nokia Theatre, where I was approached by a woman who identified herself as a personal assistant of Serena Williams. "Serena wondered if you had time to meet with her," she said.

I would've leapt at that opportunity to meet Serena even if she hadn't been rocking a low-cut, pink minidress that made a wrestling singlet look baggy by comparison.

"Why, yes," I replied. "I'd like that very much." I

had just come off the stage after accepting the Jimmy V Award for Perseverance. As the title of that trophy suggests, and despite it being one year after my home life had degenerated to the point where I vowed to quit wrestling to help my family, I hadn't given up, after all. I ended up having a dominant senior year, which resulted in a *Tonight Show* appearance; two ESPYs (I also won Best Male Athlete with a Disability, but I don't talk about that one as much); and a nice jump start to my budding career as a motivational speaker.

At 5'10", Serena had four inches on me *before* stepping into the four-inch heels she chose for the ESPYs. That put me at about eye-level with her, um, clavicles. "I just wanted to tell you that I really liked your story," she told me, once we'd been introduced. While thanking her for the compliment, and during the small talk that followed, I was careful to look her directly in the eye.

I met a lot of really cool people that night—Jason Kidd, Dirk Nowitzki, and Shawn Marion of the Dallas Mavericks; Aaron Rodgers of the Green Bay Packers; NBA Rookie of the Year Blake Griffin—all of whom congratulated me, and had nice things to say about my brief acceptance speech. At the end of the talk, I recited a poem written for the occasion by my speech coach, Dan Clark. This is how we brought it home:

"And now, as I go forward with so much more to do, this is my message:

Every soul who comes to earth
With a leg—or two—at birth
Must wrestle his opponents knowing
It's not what is, it's what *can be* that measures worth.
Make it hard, just make it possible
And through pain I'll not complain,
My spirit is unconquerable.
Fearless I will face each foe, for I know
I am capable. I don't care what's probable.
Through blood, sweat, and tears
I am Unstoppable."

THE following spring, I got a medal for courage at the National Wrestling Hall of Fame in Stillwater, Oklahoma. It was like walking around a kind of Mount Olympus for wrestlers. Dan Gable was there, as was John Smith and a host of other Hall of Famers. But I got the biggest kick out of meeting Dan Hodge, a three-time NCAA champion who is basically the John Heisman of our sport. Every year, the Dan Hodge Award goes to the NCAA's Most Outstanding Wrestler.

Even before I met Mr. Hodge, I knew all about him. He's famous for his ferociously strong grip. My high school coach, Bobby Williams, insisted that I develop extraordinary grip strength and frequently cited Dan Hodge and his ability to crush various items—apples, pliers, the bones of his opponents—with his bare hands.

He's still got it, by the way. Even at the age of eighty, Mr. Hodge was still strong enough to hurt my hand when he shook it.

I was flattered that he knew about me, too. He'd been following my career and saw me wrestle in the NCAA championships. At one point, this tough, kind old warrior looked me in the eye and said, "You're the toughest man upstairs I've ever met."

It was one of the nicest compliments I've ever gotten. It was Mr. Hodge's way of telling me I am unstoppable.

But I'm also human. Unstoppable doesn't mean I was never defeated or that I never despaired. It just means I never *stayed* defeated or gave in to despair. I've had some success because I've also experienced more than my share of failure. The trick is to take it in stride, learn from it, and focus on the next step. Smile and keep moving forward. Come on upstairs and I'll share what I've learned on the journey so far.

CHAPTER 1

I Want to See My Son

JUDY Ochoa was the youngest of Marc and Becky Ochoa's five children. She was a happy, rambunctious, slightly headstrong child, and a very good student. After finishing eighth grade with straight A's, she earned a $500 scholarship to attend St. Paul High School—a prestigious private Catholic school in Santa Fe Springs, California. Her parents were strict, but it didn't matter much. "I was a teenager," says my mother, looking back. "I was gonna figure out a way to do what I wanted to do." Have I mentioned that she's headstrong?

She was doing well and had lots of friends at school, but around the time she was fifteen, she fell in with a crowd that her parents weren't crazy about. One night after leaving a party, she caught the eye of some guy from a nearby high school who was getting in a car with some friends. They smiled at each other, chatted, and exchanged numbers. They talked a few days later and went out on a couple of dates, and then Judy went to see him play in a football game at his high school. That was the night she found out that he had a girlfriend. By that time, she was already pregnant.

My biological father was only a year or two older than she was and disappeared from her life as soon as he found out she was going to have a baby. I've never met him. About a year after I was born, he called my mom's house and asked to speak with her. Judy picked up, by chance, and recognized his voice. Pretending to be one of her sisters, she told him she wasn't home. She didn't see the point in talking to him just then, she explains. She was seventeen. He has never been in my life.

Mom was scared to be pregnant, and embarrassed and ashamed, although it wouldn't have been like her to let anyone know that. She's a strong, proud woman. Hers was a deeply Catholic family. In her community, at her Catholic school, there was serious stigma attached to bearing a child out of wedlock. Yet Judy chose to live with that stigma, to endure the stares and gossip. She never once considered having an abortion.

Early in her pregnancy, my grandparents, Marc and Becky, sat down with her. "You know what we believe," they told her, "but ultimately, the decision is yours to make."

My mother never hesitated. "That was a live person—a little baby who's part of me," she says now. "I couldn't do anything to harm it. It wouldn't be fair."

Her parents were loving, supportive, and devastated, all at once. Their baby—their bright, beautiful sixteen-year-old—was having a baby, much too early in her life. They'd had sky-high expectations for her—hopes that would now be much harder to fulfill. "I cried a lot," Becky remembers, "but that was something we had to accept. We tried to be as positive as we could." She took my mom to regular appointments with her ob-gyn, the wonderful Dr. Azmath Qureshi. Becky organized a big baby shower for my mother.

My mom had a rough spring semester: morning sickness and fatigue in high school; whispers behind her back. Even now, knowing how it all turned out, my heart goes out to her. She didn't put on much weight during her pregnancy, but people certainly knew. And they talked.

As her due date approached, I wasn't turning in the womb. I was breech, having apparently decided to make a foot-first entrance into the world. So the doctors advised a caesarian section. The anesthesiologist didn't knock my mother out for the operation, but Judy was numb from the neck down.

AND so, on the morning of July 20, 1988, I was born. Of course, Dr. Qureshi, who delivered me, noticed that I was missing a leg, but she didn't say anything—at least not to my mother. She went out to find my grandparents in the waiting room and said ominously, "There's a problem." She led them into a room, separate from the nursery, where I lay on a little bed. As she pulled back the sheet, my poor grandfather nearly fainted. He became extremely light-headed, forcing Becky and Dr. Qureshi to find him a chair.

"Do you want me to tell her?" the doctor asked my grandparents, once the color returned to Marc's face. "Or would you like to tell her yourselves?"

"I'll tell her," said Becky. Both she and Marc were crying when they entered the recovery room, where their daughter lay on a gurney, groggy with anesthetic. "That kind of woke me up a little bit," my mom remembers.

"You had a baby boy," Becky told her daughter, "but there's something we want to tell you about him." When her own children were small, and asked her where babies came from, Becky would tell them they'd been sitting on a bench in heaven, and that God decided which family to send them to.

"God had this baby sitting on a little bench in heaven, missing a leg, and He chose our family to take care of this boy."

Marc was more to the point: "He's missing his *piernita*"—his little leg.

My mother's response was visceral, primal: "I want to see my son."

"He was a beautiful little boy, and precious, just precious," she recalled for a reporter in 2011. "I didn't see his disability, I saw my son, a part of me."

In the hours and days that followed, Judy was approached by several well-intentioned people who congratulated her on giving birth, and asked how she was feeling. Adorable as I was, she was told that a special-needs child is always a far greater burden. And she was *so young*, with her whole life ahead of her. Had she considered putting me up for adoption? She shut them down immediately. Not happening. End of discussion.

My mom was all-in with me, from the beginning. She talks about not seeing my disability, looking past it, but there's no doubt that my missing leg fired some primal impulse deep inside her—kind of a maternal instinct on steroids. I mean, in those first few days, she didn't want people to see me. She hid me from sight, or kept me swaddled in a blanket. Mom was worried that if people saw that I was different, they'd think of me differently, treat me differently. She was already determined that I would lead a normal life, that I wouldn't be excluded, that I would not receive, or need, special treatment. She was just a kid herself, but she intuitively understood that the best way to protect me was by not always protecting me. She knew that the fewer limits she set for me, and that I set for myself, the happier I would be.

Of all her siblings, Mom was closest to her brother, Andy, who was just a year older. They grew up in a nice split-level house on Bluefield Avenue in La Mirada. They had a backyard pool and a park nearby. My mother loved that house, and has said that if she could move anywhere, she'd move back there. She tagged along with Andy, rode bikes with him, played baseball in the park with him and his friends. She was a tomboy, which helps explain why it wasn't really in her nature to be overly protective of me. She didn't believe in sheltering or confining me.

I slept in a crib in my mom's room. With Becky generously providing child care, Judy went back to high school for her senior year. Mom, as I mentioned, was all-in, fully embracing the idea of raising a child . . . in theory. But the reality was that she was only sixteen years old and was somewhat unclear on the concept of being a mom. It took Judy a few months to fully grasp the scope of her new responsibility. With built-in baby-sitting from my grandparents (thanks again, Becky and Marc!), she kept an active social life. But things came to a head one night when my mom and some girlfriends were "cruising" Whittier Boulevard. My mother lost track of her friends, and ended up zipping up and down the avenue on the back of some guy's motorcycle. At 2:00 in the morning she had to call her dad for a ride home. Just as Marc arrived, this James Dean wannabe popped a wheelie, then went speeding into the night.

My grandfather was not pleased.

When my mom came down to breakfast the next morning, her folks were sitting at the kitchen table, waiting for her. They made her an offer. She was still a young girl, they told her. Perhaps she was too young to take on the burden of motherhood. They offered to adopt me, and raise me as her brother.

It was a pivotal moment in my mother's life. She gave their offer some thought, but said no. "It was like a switch flipped for her," Becky remembers. "He's my son, it's up to me to raise him," Judy replied. "He's a part of me."

While there were still some "ups and downs," Becky recalls, that was the morning, the moment, that Judy started to settle down, and step up to the job of being my mom.

MY mom became fiercely protective of me. She would get angry when people stared at me, and give them dirty looks. Nor did she appreciate it much if they tried to do something special for me. In Judy's eyes, such gestures—no matter how well-intentioned—called attention to the fact that I was different. She also bristled when people asked her if it was "okay" to hold me. She got that a lot. There's something about being a one-legged infant that makes people hesitant to pick you up.

Maybe they were worried I was super fragile, like a China doll or something. Maybe they thought if they held me incorrectly, my other leg might fall off. Of course they meant no disrespect, but it still bugged Judy. If you looked at her baby the wrong way, she was ready to get all up in your face. Finally her own mother told her that it was natural for people to be curious, and maybe a little alarmed by or scared of a baby with a missing limb. She encouraged her daughter to be less defensive and angry, and I have to say, with the exception of several truly epic verbal takedowns, my mother has been.

Early in my NCAA final match with Iowa's Matt McDonough in 2011, the ESPN announcers spent a lot of time talking about my "vise-like grip." (While they were talking about it, I used that grip to get McDonough in a cross-wrist hold that helped me score a couple points.) I spent a lot of time, once I started wrestling, working on tensile, or "grip" strength. I squeezed a tennis ball all day long, hung on the climbing wall at my high school until my forearms burned with lactic acid. At a sporting goods store, I found a grip-strengthening contraption called a Wrist Machine.

I don't know if it was my unconscious way of compensating for a missing leg, but I've always had that strength. I used it to crawl up the side of my crib, to pull myself up the cargo netting at the playland in McDonald's. While a lot of babies are crawling by their seventh or eighth month, that's when I started "scooting"—pulling myself along with my arms. Most kids walk around their first birthday; that's when I started hopping. My grandmother still finds it incredible, but really, what else was I going to do?

Years later, after I started making a name for myself in my sport, Andy remembered that his kid sister, my mother, used to wrestle with me when I was still just a toddler. To this day, he is surprised by how rambunctious this horseplay sometimes got. Even when I took a hard fall, he and Judy recall, I always bounced up with a big grin on my face, ready for more. I think the reason for that roughhousing was that my mother was trying to toughen me up, getting me ready for the rough-and-tumble of the outside world. She knew a one-legged boy wasn't going to have an easy go of it.

To raise me, my mother ended up dropping out of high school a few months before graduation. She didn't go to college. And yet, she's one of the smartest people I know. For a teenage girl, she did an amazing, instinctive job walking the fine line between protecting me like a lioness, and at the same time nudging me out into the world, exposing me to pain and failure, because she knew I was going to have to cope with those things. The bond between us has always been extraordinarily strong. It sounds like a good thing, but it bugged the crap out of the next guy she ended up dating.

HIS name was Ron. He was a handsome, charismatic nineteen-year-old when my mother got involved with him. He was also a controlling, jealous, self-absorbed serial philanderer who was married to another woman, with whom he had two children. But he told Judy over and over how much he loved her. They started going out.

My grandparents were strongly opposed to the relationship—imagine that! Marc in particular had an instant, visceral dislike of Ron. But Mom has that stubborn streak. Rather than listen to her father, she vowed to prove him wrong. So, when I was two, we moved in with Ron, who almost immediately set about proving my grandfather correct. Even as he initiated divorce proceedings from his first wife, Ron stayed in touch with a third woman, an ex-girlfriend. That was the woman Ron's mother described to her new daughter-in-law as her son's true "soul mate." That was one of the women with whom he cheated throughout his marriage to my mother.

Right from the start, Ron resented the time my mom spent with me, and the attention she paid to me. Maybe the sight of my face reminded him that my mother had been with another guy before she was with him.

Not to say that there weren't good times with Ron. On Sunday afternoons we would barbecue, then sit around as a family, watching the Raiders game. Countless times, we sat on the couch and watched *Rocky*, or the classic wrestling movie *Vision Quest*. When I was ten he would drive me forty-five minutes to the Gracie Jiu-Jitsu Academy in Phoenix. It was our thing. I loved him. But it got harder and harder to respect him. He had a lot of good qualities, but he wasn't kind to my mother. He was unclear on the concept of monogamy, and there were times the mere sight of me was enough to put him in a very dark place.

Even when I'm not saying much, or *anything*, Judy is able to read me: She can tell from my body language or if my jaw is clenched whether I'm happy or upset. The reason for that is that we'd had to learn to communicate silently, because it often made Ron angry when we spoke to each other. Many of their most heated arguments centered around me. Just when my mother was close to leaving Ron and moving back in with her parents—"to clean up the mess I'd made," she recalls—she discovered that she was pregnant.

She stayed with Ron and they were married in December 1991. In the years ahead, he would abuse her and cheat on her more times than my mother could count. He never tired of telling Judy that her close relationship with me was sick and unnatural. He got that exactly wrong—the bond between us is a beautiful thing. My mother's love and strength were, and are, my salvation.

AROUND the time I was three my mom started driving me the twenty-two miles from our house to the Shriners Hospital for Children in Los Angeles. I don't remember my stepdad coming on those trips, but I do recall that the hospital was a great big building with lots of giant toys inside. I went there to be fitted for a prosthetic leg. Because I was born without a hip socket, doctors attached the leg to a bowl-like object. I would sit in the bowl, which was then strapped to me with Velcro. The prosthesis was heavy, awkward, and took a long time to put on and take off. It felt like I was dragging around a big piece of wood—which I was. I felt like Pinocchio. It was uncomfortable and I truly despised it.

But the fittings and the materials and labor—all donated by the Shriners—were expensive. For me to just stash it in the closet would've seemed ungrateful. So I was expected to wear it. Mom would set up a kind of circuit in our house: I'd start in the kitchen, then go clomping down the hallway to the living room, around the sofa, back up the hall to the dining room, and back to the kitchen. She'd make me do the loop five or ten times to get used to the leg. I was just a little kid who wanted to get around as fast as I could and I came to see the prosthetic as this odd-looking anchor. An anchor that *pinched*. So I would unstrap it and ditch it every chance I got. Or I'd tell my mom I had to go to the bathroom—even if I didn't—because that meant the leg would have to come off. It was such a hassle to strap the thing back on that she often lacked the energy to do so. By the time I was seven, I'd worn her down: She basically left it up to me whether I wanted to keep wearing it. Good-bye, prosthetic leg.

Between scooting, crutching, army crawling, and riding a bike (with one of those caged pedals that held my foot in place), I got around just about as well as most other kids—and better than some. When I was five I put a scare into my mother by shimmying up a fifty-foot pole in a park behind our house, and sitting in the birdbath on top of it.

My mom protected me, but at the same time she knew when, and how far, to back off. She knew that kids could be mean, and came to realize that she was helpless to prevent them from teasing me and ostracizing me. She recalls the day I returned from kindergarten, dropped my crutches, and threw my arms around her waist, sobbing. She always told me, "This is the way God made you," and on that afternoon I kept asking, "WHY did He make me this way?"

It crushed her to see me crying; she had guilt—still has it, she recently admitted to me—that my missing limb is somehow her fault. But she hid those feelings from me, assured me everything would be okay, that I was normal. Despite the hardships she's endured in her

UNSTOPPABLE

life—and despite the recent performances of the Oakland Raiders, of whom she is a lifelong fan—my mom is an incurable optimist. (She had to be, really, to stay in her marriage as long as she did.)

She knew she couldn't protect me from cruel, ignorant people. What she could do, and did all the time, was support me, be there for me, smile at me, and tell me, "You're okay. There's nothing wrong with you. God made you this way for a reason."

Looking back on it, I'm in awe of her strength—and strength of will. Regardless of the storms raging in her marriage, she put that turmoil in a compartment, shielding us from the worst of it. So even if I couldn't puzzle out the "reason" the Creator had sent me into the world with an odd number of limbs, I wasn't a scared, anxious kid. Heck, I probably should have been *more* afraid. But as I told Jay Leno, I thought I was Superman. With my mother, there was never any doubt that everything was going to work out.

CHAPTER 2

You're Not My Son

WE weren't refugees, exactly, but we sure got around. I moved eight or nine times before I got to high school. It was a challenge, making friends whenever we pulled up stakes, but that was okay, because my siblings and I had one another. I had—okay, *have*—a fairly extensive Teenage Mutant Ninja Turtle collection, although my passion for those amphibians cooled once I got turned on to the X-Men. I was a serious X-Men geek; I liked Gambit the best. If you're familiar with that Marvel Comics series, you'll recognize Gambit as the mutant who throws the cards. He's an orphan and a loner with superhuman strength whose real name is Remy LeBeau.

(I'm currently the proud owner of two rottweilers: Remy and Beast.)

I loved superheroes. Truth be told, when I let my imagination run, which was often, I *was* one. My brothers and our friends and I were always battling with plastic swords. Running around the neighborhood with my sword and special backpack containing such superhero accessories as a pocketknife, flashlight, and cap gun, I felt indestructible.

When I say "running," I mean that I was locomoting myself with the help of crutches. I'm not gonna lie, I could *really* get along on my sticks. And when we were on bikes, it was no problem. I had my own sweet ride, a black bike with green trim and a little rocket on the side. When I was first learning to ride, we didn't bother with training wheels. At the suggestion of my grandfather, we installed a "closed" pedal on the left side—the kind that holds your foot in place (but also lets you pull your foot out). Judy decked me out in a helmet, elbow pads, knee pad, and chest protector. I looked like a little riot policeman. I was fine going straight, and turning left. Right turns were a problem: When I leaned into the turn, I was missing the counterweight to pull out of the turn. So I got really good at pushing the eject button—jumping off the bike just before it crashed.

Those were the days before I started to really notice girls, before my missing leg made me feel acutely self-conscious at school. When I was younger, it actually didn't seem like that big a deal, because of how casually my parents and sibs treated me. I had some rude awakenings, but not too many.

There was that morning on the playground on the first day of school when I was in third grade. I wanted to play with some kids by the tire swing, but one of the boys said he didn't want to play with me because I only had one leg. It's funny how things work out, though. That kid, Victor, became one of my two best friends that year, along with Hector. We were like the Three Musketeers. Victor, as you can probably tell, didn't always engage his brain before he spoke. He was fiery and quick-tempered, with a haircut like Wolverine's. Hector was mellower, taller than both of us, with short, almost shaved, hair.

I'd ditch my crutches at recess to play football. Then the bell would ring, and I could never remember where I'd left them, so I'd be hopping around the field looking for them, with those guys helping me. Life outside the house was pretty carefree. I didn't think that much about the limb I didn't have.

That started to change in middle school, the years when the ante is raised, it seems, when boys and girls are becoming adolescents and taking a more active interest in each other. It's around this time that the consequences for being different, for failing to blend in, are more severe. For the first time in my life, I started thinking that, yeah, there was something wrong with me.

Making my away through the corridors of my middle school, I became acutely aware of the fact that my crutches made a clicking sound, announcing my approach. After that I made an effort to somehow crutch around more quietly. The last thing I wanted to do was stick out.

I had crushes on girls, but was *much* too shy to act on them. The odds of rejection were so high, I feared, that I chose not to make myself any more vulnerable than I already felt. I remember my mom telling me how handsome I looked as she dropped me off for the sixth-grade Valentine's formal at Ramona Middle School in La Verne, California, where I spent the next three hours standing in a corner, talking to my fellow wallflowers while our more outgoing classmates had a blast.

"How was the dance?" Mom asked me when I got home.

"I'm never going to another dance as long as I live," I replied.

(I would break that vow my freshman year in college. I was dating a high school senior who asked me to her prom. Because I really liked her, I said yes. Problem was, I had no idea how to slow dance, which is how I came to be standing one evening with my hands on the waist of fellow wrestler Wes Fimbrez as he talked me through a basic two-step. The lesson was a success: At the prom, I slow danced to "Better Days," by the Goo Goo Dolls. By pinching my crutches up under my arms, I was able to move with the music *and* hold my date. That tune became our song, until she dusted me a few months later.)

By taking *very few* chances—the complete opposite of my wrestling style—I created a little safety zone around myself. By making myself an island, I was signing up for extended periods of loneliness. I didn't really have a girlfriend all through middle school and high school. Yes, there was this nice stretch of time in seventh grade when I got kind of close to a cute, short brunette named Tanya. We'd meet before school to talk. We walked to class together and ate lunch together. But we never got together outside of school.

Fitting in was everything. That's why I loved playing flag football in sixth and seventh grade. I was a safety, hopping around, having a blast, actually making a play here and there. Being a member of a team, being one of the guys, meant a lot to me. I wanted to be a part of some collective—to not be an outcast. I wanted to feel like I belonged. Sadly, that wasn't something I could take for granted, even in my own home.

I was nine years old when my stepdad rocked my world. We were sitting in the van outside a beauty salon in Safford, Arizona, waiting for my mom. I was in the backseat, my little brother Nicholas asleep next to me. Ron started talking to me, telling me a story about his own stepdad. And then he dropped a bomb on me:

"I'm not your real dad. We don't know where your real dad is, but if you want to find him, we can find him."

I don't recall him saying it in a way that was intentionally hurtful. Nor did he say it in a loving way. He was straight to the point, his usual, blunt self.

I heard the words, but they didn't sink in right away. The news was literally unbelievable to me. Ron had come into the picture when I was two, and I had no memory of life without him. To hear this at the age of nine, after I'd thought of him as my dad for my whole life, leveled me. I lost my bearings, started seeing my life in a different light. I wasn't sure how to act around him, or how to interpret his words and actions. From then on out, when I did something wrong, and he disciplined me, I would think, *He's being harder on me 'cause I'm not his kid.* It felt like his love for me was different. It started to feel like I was a guest in my own house.

Not that I was able to articulate any of this at the time. I learned early on to turn my face into a mask, to put my emotions in a box and just . . . shut down. *Mom and Dad are screaming at each other? Dad has left us again, without saying where he's going, or when he'll be back? We need to pack up our stuff because we're moving to a new place, again?* I became a master, in the face of every kind of drama, at pretending nothing was happening. As I got older, and finally started getting a few dates, this proved to be a problem. More than once, I've heard this from a woman I care about: "You never let me know how you're feeling." And they were right. It's something I'm working on.

The news that Ron wasn't my biological father explained something for me. I'd always noticed that I was a lot darker than my sister and three brothers. Funny thing is, despite us looking nothing alike, I never suspected that Ron wasn't my dad, probably the same way Will Ferrell's character never reflects on why he's so much bigger than his coworkers in the movie *Elf.* My biological father was black and Ron is Hispanic. My being half-black didn't go over so well with some of the people on Ron's side of the family. "They were prejudiced," says my mother. She recalls the reaction of Ron's mother, the first time she laid eyes on me: "He'll never be my grandchild."

"If you can't accept him," Judy replied, "you're not going to have a relationship with any of my kids."

My mom doesn't deal in empty threats. Growing up, we saw very little of that side of the family, although I did notice that, after I showed up on the ESPYs, a bunch of my cousins from my stepfather's side of the family started hitting me up on Facebook.

Other things made more sense once I learned that Ron wasn't my biological father. Talking to my mother, he would refer to the other children as "our children," then refer to me as "your son." Sometimes I'd be out in the yard, and see them arguing through the window. I'd hear my name, and my stepdad would be looking out at me with an angry expression on his face. They fought a lot, and a lot of the time they were fighting about me. When I'd come home from college, then sit down to catch up with my mother, I could see his mood darken. He begrudged me that time, that intimacy, with her. He told her it was "a sick relationship," and told me I was too much of a "mama's boy."

My mom pleaded with him to legally adopt me, but Ron never did. I found out later that he didn't even want me to have his name. But it meant a lot to my mom that my surname was Robles. When I was thirteen, and without Ron's approval, she filed paperwork and took me to the courthouse, where my name was legally changed to Robles. My mother had four children with Ron: my sister, Ronnie; and my brothers Nicholas, Joshua, and Andrew. It meant a lot to my mother that all of us—her and all of her kids—share the same name. In her mind, it's a kind of glue that binds us. (And believe me, that's the *only* reason she's kept her married name all these years.)

She definitely didn't do it to honor her husband—who, as it happened, had recently left her for another woman . . . again. As usual, he came groveling back, apologizing, asking forgiveness. My mom took him back; that's how desperate she was to keep the family intact.

ALTHOUGH we lived like nomads, moving into a new house or apartment every couple years, there was one constant in our lives: On fall Sundays, we blocked out four hours to watch the Raiders game. It's strictly a family deal. I've had to explain to several girlfriends that it just wouldn't be a good idea for me to include them. They don't always understand. I tell them, for instance, that before kickoffs we all stand and hold hands. Most of us have Raider tattoos, including my mother. That logo—the crossed swords behind the helmeted man with the eye patch—is kind of our family crest.

Go ahead, pile on. Trust me, we've heard worse. We'll always love the Raiders, even as they find new and creative ways to break our hearts. Indeed, I am working on this chapter on a day when Oakland coughed up a two-touchdown lead in the final eight minutes against the Detroit Lions.

I gave real football a shot in ninth grade. In the summer before that school year, we had moved to Mesa, Arizona, where I played for the freshman team. As a one-legged, ninety-pound defensive tackle, I was, not surprisingly, overmatched. I wasn't having fun, the way I'd enjoyed flag football. I wasn't that good, and my coaches and teammates took it easy on me. I wanted to earn their praise because I was a good football player. Instead, I felt like the handicapped kid. I was getting special treatment.

People meant well, but it sucked the enjoyment out of the experience for me. So that ended up being my last year of football, a sport I still love. Football made me realize that I didn't mind—in fact, I rather enjoyed—violent physical contact. Plus, hopping around with about twenty pounds of gear made my leg a lot stronger, which ended up being a big help in my new sport.

Before moving into our house in Mesa, we lived for a couple months with my maternal grandparents in Tucson. My cousin Jesse wrestled for Salpointe High in Tucson, and invited me to tag along and watch the team during summer workouts. I'd always enjoyed mixing it up with my brothers and cousins—roughhousing, grappling, general horseplay—and I liked UFC fighting (Mixed Martial Arts). My stepdad had even taken me to some Brazilian jiujitsu classes when I was ten. "You'd be good at wrestling," Jesse told me. "You're little, but you're strong."

He explained that the sport was broken up into weight classes, so you only had to go up against guys your size. I tagged along with him for a few practices. My intention was to do some push-ups and sit-ups to get stronger for football. But I ended up just watching the practice, studying what they were doing, how they were moving around on the mat. I have to be honest, it didn't seem like fun. On my third day, when the coach asked me if I wanted to try it, I said no. I told him I didn't really feel like it.

That's when Jesse walked over and went into his used-car-salesman mode. "You could be *good* at this," he said. "You've got the build. You already like to mix it up. In this sport you don't get in trouble when you body-slam or choke someone—that's what you're supposed to do!"

"All right, whatever," I said. "I'll give it a try." They threw me in with a little guy who beat me pretty good. But I scrapped with him, rolling around, fighting back. I didn't know what I was doing, and he kept putting me on my back. But by the end of the session I was exhausted, and exhilarated. I walked away with a spark for the sport. From that day on, I read as much as I could about it, watched video of it, talked to wrestlers.

I liked the idea of going up against guys my size. I liked the emphasis on strength, fitness, and strategy. I liked that there was a direct link between how hard you worked and how well you did. I sensed that this was a sport that might give me my best chance to show what I had—to show the size of my heart. The day I first went out on the mat, I was still smiling at dinnertime.

My mom had told me a thousand times that "God made you this way for a reason." That day, He gave me a glimpse of just what that reason was.

MESA Junior High was in a gritty neighborhood on the west side, across the street from a couple of Mexican food joints and a gun shop. After school there would be fights; I'd see guys get jumped. There wasn't a wrestling room, per se: We used the football team's weight room. Before practice, we moved the weights to the side, then rolled out the mat. After practice we rolled up the mat and put the weights back.

I wasn't very good—I was scrappy and willing. I just had no idea what I was doing. I wasn't . . . good. Later, when my path crossed with an exceptionally talented coach, I learned to drop down low on the mat, where I was much more dangerous. In ninth grade, I still hadn't figured that out. I stood up, like everybody else. I had pretty good balance, but I couldn't attack, couldn't take my shots—that's the name for those lightning strikes a wrestler takes at his opponent's legs. I wasn't dangerous. I had no identity, no style. I might as well have been one of those guys I'd seen brawling in the street.

It didn't help that the lowest weight class was 103 pounds. I was ninety pounds, dripping wet. I'd weigh in wearing my warm-ups, kneepad, headgear, and shoe, and with a bottle of water in my pocket, and still have eight pounds to spare.

I'm sure that's part of the reason that a lady in the bleachers started laughing at me before the first match I ever wrestled. Our team jogged out and circled the mat, with me crutching right along with them. Too nervous to sit, my mom watched from the edge of the bleachers. She was stunned to see this woman looking at me, along with some students of the school we were visiting, and cracking up. My mother is a gentle woman, and deeply Christian, but that lady has no idea how close she came to a trip to the emergency room that afternoon. Instead, Mom got up in her face and asked forcefully, "What the heck is wrong with you? That's my son you're laughing at. Do you see something funny?"

The woman mumbled something about how she thought I was making a joke—that I wasn't really a wrestler. Judy told her she should be ashamed of herself, and walked away.

That woman was in the distinct minority. Often, after I wrestled, perfect strangers would approach me, some with tears in their eyes. They wanted to shake my hand, maybe take a picture with me. I was conflicted about that kind of attention. Remember, I was still just trying to blend in, trying to impress some girl—any girl—enough to hold hands with me after school. I didn't want to be recognized as something special if I hadn't actually done anything special. At the same time, to hear someone I'd never met before talking about how much I'd inspired him—that made me feel pretty good about myself.

I lost eight of my thirteen matches that year. Our season ended with a citywide tournament. I'd be wrestling the 103-pounders from the other six junior high schools in the city—the same guys I'd be competing with the following year at Mesa High. My first match was against some kid who, like me, had yet to learn the finer points of the sport. We basically fought without using our fists. At one point I tried to tackle him, as if I were still playing football. At the last moment, he lowered his head, and I bloodied my mouth on his skull. But I won! I came off the mat with a huge grin on my face, my teeth all red, blood on my singlet. My mom was all worried about the blood, but I was just ecstatic to get a win.

I came in fifth out of six in the tournament, but still got a medal. I was *pumped*. Just as exciting as getting a medal was meeting the man who handed it to me. Bob Williams is the wrestling coach at Mesa High, where I'd be a sophomore the following year. He's highly respected all over the state. He looked me in the eye, shook my hand, and said, "Good job." And all I could think of afterward was, *I can't wait to wrestle for him.*

I knew he could help me. I had no idea how much.

CHAPTER 3

Take a Knee

BACK when I was losing more matches than I won, people congratulated me for trying hard. They patted me on the back "for just being out here." I'm grateful to them for their encouragement. However, as I developed into a competent wrestler, and then a dominant one, reactions were more varied and I attracted a group of skeptics. In the "comments" sections of online articles and discussion threads on wrestling websites, my detractors argued that, as a one-legged wrestler, I had a distinct advantage. *My opponents had one fewer of my limbs to grab onto. How was that fair?* Plus, I possessed the upper-body strength of a wrestler from a higher weight class. As one aggrieved poster put it, "I think [he] should have to wear a prosthetic and weigh in with it."

"Man, does he have a crazy advantage," added another. "His body allows him to have so much more muscle mass because of his missing leg."

Reading those remarks, you would have thought there were wrestlers all over the country damning their luck that they'd been born with both legs.

That missing leg didn't seem like much of an advantage when I was getting pinned every other match in ninth grade, though. I tried to let those comments roll off my back, but honestly, they pissed me off. They insinuated that I was somehow winning with trickery or deceit; that I had some magical shortcut. Yes, by the time I was seventeen or so, I was powerfully built. That's not because I woke up one morning and decided to be ripped. It was because I busted my butt, nine to ten months out of the year. People who say I had an unfair advantage because I've only got one leg didn't see me out in the Mesa High parking lot in hundred-degree-plus heat, pushing my car over a bunch of speed bumps, until that leg buckled from exhaustion.

Those people never met Chris Freije, my MHS Jackrabbit teammate. Chris was this mild-mannered guy in wire-rimmed glasses who looked like he lived in the science building. But once he stepped onto the mat, a kind of Dr. Bruce Banner/Incredible Hulk metamorphosis took place. He turned into some gonzo, wild-eyed

152-pound ball of anger and aggression. At that time, he was honing the take-no-prisoners style that would win him the state championship (and earn him, incidentally, more misconducts than anyone in the history of Mesa High wrestling). It was Chris who would sit in the driver's seat screaming words of encouragement (if you could call it that), as I hopped behind the car, pushing it over those speed bumps; Chris who explained to me early on, "Before you get better, we're gonna break you down so bad you've got nowhere else to go."

But first he had to notice me. First he had to learn my name.

THE word went out before my sophomore year: Anyone interested in wrestling for the varsity was invited to participate in unofficial summer workouts. So I stopped by the high school, and entered the room that would be my sanctuary and prison for the next three years. The high school team had its own dedicated wrestling room, with an adjoining weight room. No more rolling up the mats after practice. I was moving up in the world!

The first day I dropped in, I wrestled a guy named Ryan Hatch, who was stronger than me and had more experience. But I was fighting hard. While we tangled, an upperclassman appeared, hovering over us, offering me little pieces of advice. It was Freije. He wasn't the most talented wrestler in the room, either, but he was the most respected. He was scrappy, tenacious, and (once he stepped onto the mat) mean. He saw something in me that reminded him of himself. Despite the two-year age difference, we hit it off. Chris became a kind of mentor to me.

His father, Dave, had wrestled in college back in Indiana and now coached wrestling, but not at Mesa High. As a small boy, Chris would get dropped off wherever his dad was working. Instead of going to day care, he'd hang out in the wrestling room. Chris had been around the sport most of his life, and had an endless supply of drills and workouts, all of them designed, it seemed, to bring us to our breaking point.

He also worked out at a nearby Gold's Gym, and often took me along. We'd suffer through whatever sadistic circuit workout Freije concocted, then hit the sauna. I ended up spending a lot of time in saunas over the next eight years. But I'd never been in one until I went to Freije's gym. The first time I walked through that door, the air stung my lungs. After about a minute, it was so hot I started to panic. I stood up to get out and he blocked the door. "Can't leave until we've done a workout," he explained. For neither the first nor the last time I thought, *This guy is out of his freaking mind.* Two hundred sit-ups and fifty push-ups later, I finally got out of there. I've been in a lot of saunas since then, but none have ever felt hotter.

Haunting the wrestling room during those summer

sessions, stealing glances from his office or taking a knee in a corner of the room, was a dark-haired man who didn't say much, even as he appeared to take everything in. Bob Williams wrestled for the Jackrabbits in the mid-seventies. Since returning to his alma mater in 1992, he's coached Mesa High to three team titles, along the way producing twenty or so state champions. I got great coaching at Arizona State, but Bob Williams was the best coach I will ever have.

He wasn't a screamer. He's actually a gentle soul who prefers not to raise his voice. When he did, you knew you'd better hang on every syllable. It's easy for me to say that now, with benefit of hindsight. But the truth is, when he offered me an important piece of advice that first season—it ended up being the suggestion that changed the direction of my life—I resisted it. I wanted nothing to do with it.

"**IF** you came out for wrestling to get your name in the paper, you picked the wrong sport." That was Coach's message to us during one of our first team meetings. The newspaper headlines, he told us, tended to go to the football and basketball teams. But we would outwork those guys, he promised. And 99 percent of that work would go unnoticed by the outside world. But we would know. The band of brothers who sat in that room and toughed it out together—we would know.

That sat just fine with me. I was fifteen years old, with far less experience than almost everyone else in the room. I felt invisible and, frankly, wanted to *stay* invisible, while I got a few things figured out. I was not invisible to Coach. There were times that first year when it felt like I was the only guy he could see.

Bob also wrestled at Arizona State. His coach there was the legendary Bobby Douglas, a five-time national champion and an icon in the sport. One of Douglas's bedrock principles was to protect your legs at all cost. Now Williams applied that commandment to me. I'd spent my first season hopping around the mat, basically begging opponents to attack my leg. Which they often did. Early on, before the season had even started, Coach wanted me to get off my foot, to get down on the mat, to take a knee. That way, he said, I'd be presenting my opponent a smaller target, and I could protect my leg, concealing a weakness, while emphasizing my upper body, a strength. Of course, as a runt sophomore, I was still a string bean in a singlet. But here was something to build on, something I'd lacked as a freshman. Coach was giving me the foundation for a style, the beginnings of an identity. But it was a unique style, a style that called attention to my missing leg, the thing that made me different from everyone. And for a long time, I wanted nothing to do with it.

When everyone else was doing drills standing up,

Coach W insisted that I drop to the mat. That went against the grain of my own philosophy. I was determined to go through life proving I could do everything everybody else could do. So I resisted. When the coaches told me to get down, I did so reluctantly, then popped up when they weren't looking.

Coach pushed back. He respected my determination to do the same workout everyone else was doing. But he also wanted me to win matches, and if I insisted on standing up in competition, I was going to get my lunch eaten. He deputized assistant coach Dave DiDomenico to keep an eagle eye on me during practice. If I refused to drop to the mat when instructed, Dave made me do push-ups. I came around.

I improved quickly once I started to feel more comfortable down low, close to the mat, moving around on my arms. The coaches saw potential in me—they just didn't see immediate potential. I was good, they agreed, but not as good as Joe Taylor, the other sophomore wrestling in the 103-pound weight class. "Joe had strength, balance, speed—all the tools," Coach Williams once recounted for a reporter. "We were really looking toward him. . . . Anthony, we thought, would develop toward his junior and senior years."

It threw a monkey wrench into their plans when I beat Taylor in the preseason wrestle-off that determined who would win that starting spot.

"That kind of changed our tune," Williams recalls. "We thought, 'Hey, we'd better focus more on what this kid's doing.'"

The coaches were spot-on with Joe, who did go on to be a state champion and all-American—just in a different weight class. We were workout partners for three years, and I was blessed to have him as a teammate. Joe was a precise technician, very quick, very slick. I was more brutish and scrappy. Over the course of our time in that room, we rubbed off on each other: I became a more fluid, intuitive, and (don't laugh) *artistic* wrestler, while Joe became more aggressive—even developing a bit of a mean streak.

Nothing like Freije, though.

Chris was an animal, and a territorial one at that. "You gotta act like you *own* this mat," he would tell me. "The other guy is coming out to take it from you. You've gotta do whatever you've gotta do to defend your mat, to get your hand raised at the end."

He brought an urgency to practice that made all of us better. It also made all of us a little afraid. Still, I tagged along behind him, challenging him on the mat, even though it meant that he'd flatten me like a tortilla. When we had to do bear crawls around the wrestling room, I'd wait until it was his turn to go, then follow him. As the season went on, I came closer and closer to staying with him. I can still hear Coach yelling to Chris, "He's catching you! He's catching you!"

The more he accepted and respected me, paradoxically, the more he punished me. Later that summer, when he was getting ready for college and I was preparing for my junior year, he would draw up practices designed to break me. He'd mash my face into the mat, throw me against the wall, or into the aero bikes. A few times he literally tossed me out of the wrestling room—I'd come flying through the padded double doors and into the basketball court, like an extra getting thrown out of a saloon in a Western movie.

Sometimes I'd end up crying. We wouldn't stop until I'd reached the point of failure—until I couldn't go anymore. And then I'd keep going. I'd fight back from that. The lesson was, even when you think you're done—tapped out—even when you think it's over, you still have something left.

I remember one night we'd lost a dual meet at Mountain View High. On the drive back, some of the guys were goofing off. Coach Williams didn't like the vibe and turned it into a teachable moment. Back at Mesa High, he had us all sit on the mat, then informed us we'd be taking part in an impromptu sandbag workout. It entailed reverse push-ups with sandbags on our chests. Between sets of push-ups, we jogged around the room with the sandbags, which ranged in weight from, say, twenty to thirty pounds.

My problem was that the seniors grabbed the lighter sandbags first. I ended up with a big one that weighed almost half as much as I did. The push-ups I could do, barely. But when it came time to run around the room with the sandbag, I'd hop a few steps, stumble, struggle to my feet, hop a few steps, stumble. It wasn't pretty, and I was in the way, forcing my teammates to swerve to avoid me. I didn't really care. Coach had given us instructions, and there was no way I was going to stop before everyone else stopped. I didn't notice it at the time—he's shared this with reporters since—but there was a moment he stopped talking and turned away from us, pretending to look into his office.

He had been moved to tears.

THE last time I ever stood up in a match was in a dual meet against Red Mountain High. In high school, matches consist of three two-minute periods. In the final minute against a tough, smart opponent named Greg Carbajal, I was up by two points. With thirty seconds left, he got an escape, cutting my lead to one. And just then, for some reason, I regressed to ninth grade. I stood up, hopping on my leg. Carbajal knifed in, took me down, scored two points, and won the match by one. The coaches yelled at me after that, but they didn't have to. I knew I'd screwed up.

I never stood up in a wrestling match again.

Carbajal was a problem. Dude had my number. I wrestled him again at the East Valley regional tournament, and he destroyed me. He figured out that I was weak on bottom, and turned me into a slot machine. Instead of coins, I coughed up points.

Let me explain. At the start of the second and third periods, wrestlers start either in control, on top, or without control, on bottom. (The wrestler whose turn it is to choose may also opt for "neutral"—standing up.) For reasons I'll get into later, I've always been pretty strong on top. For most of that season, I struggled on bottom. Carbajal was a skilled leg-rider—a "legger," as we say in the wrestling room. He would pinch my hips between his legs, as if he was riding a horse, and basically stretch me out until I was almost flat. I burned a lot of energy and gave up a lot of points trying to escape.

The cold truth was that he'd solved me. After edging me for victory in our dual meet, he'd blown me out in the regional tournament. The gap between us was growing. My realistic goal was to get on the podium at the state meet. But if I ran into Carbajal early, I worried, I wasn't going to even make it out of the consolation bracket.

ON a Thursday morning in February 2004, I walked into the 14,879-seat Arizona Veterans Memorial Coliseum and looked around. It took my breath away. The previous season, I'd competed in a cramped little bandbox of a wrestling room that we borrowed from the football team. Mesa Junior High was only twenty miles east, but on this day the distance felt much greater. A little over a year after finishing dead last in the Mesa city tournament for ninth graders, eight months after Ryan Hatch rag-dolled me around the room in my first summer practice, I'd qualified for the 5A state wrestling tournament. I'd won thirty-four matches in the 103-pound weight class, and lost twelve. The coaches and I had basically invented a wrestling style from scratch. It's hard to describe how far I'd come, how much I'd learned.

I had not learned, unfortunately, how to counter a strong, determined leg rider. My realistic goal for the weekend was to stand on the podium on Saturday night. That meant I needed to finish in the top six. After winning my first match, I got schooled in the second, losing 16–3 to Jesse Torres, who kicked my butt right into the consolation bracket. But I stayed alive, dominating two straight opponents. My goal, which had disappeared behind the clouds, was once again visible. To place in the state tournament, all I had to do was beat my next opponent.

It was Carbajal.

"ANTHONY, come with us."

Two hours before the match that would determine

if I would place at the state meet, Coach DiDomenico and Dave Freije motioned for me to follow them. In a room in the bowels of the arena, they'd rolled out a couple practice mats. Dave is Chris's dad, who, as it happened, had been a "legger" back in his day. He and Coach D proceeded to give me a crash course on what to do when you're stuck on the bottom against a leg rider.

Carbajal and I were tied, 2–2, after two periods. But he was starting the third period on top. Immediately, he snaked his left leg around mine and started pressing me into the mat. This time, I was expecting it. This time, I had an answer, jerking my knee up toward my chest, bowing my back and turning violently to my right, throwing my hips down and sideways. I was a bronco, basically, trying to buck a rodeo cowboy off my back.

It worked. As Carbajal slid off, I grabbed his head on the way down. *I'll take that.* With one of my elbows behind his neck and the other behind one of his knees, I brought my arms together, slowly closing the vise, squeezing him into a "cradle." I got a point for escaping, then more points for the near-fall. I beat Carbajal 7–2 that day, and never lost to him again. It was never close.

I finished the state tournament in sixth place. I was content with that—at first. "To be sixth, I feel pretty good about that," I told a reporter from the *East Valley Tribune*. "I was just happy to beat [Carbajal] once."

Sitting in the stands a few hours later, my sixth-place medal dangling from a ribbon around my neck, I started to feel less content, and more hungry. Chris was out on the mat, under the lights, going tooth and nail in the championship match for the 152-pound title. Freije had won forty-seven of his forty-eight matches that season. But he was in trouble now.

He was tangled up with Wes Pierce, a skilled, rangy wrestler who, at 6'1", gave Freije fits. They'd wrestled twice before and Chris had lost both times. Those two guys had been mixing it up since middle school. They'd wrestled on a club team together; they'd been workout partners. They knew each other's styles and setups. They knew what to expect from each other. That helped explain why there were no takedowns in the first two periods. With the score tied 2–all after three, they went into overtime, then double overtime. The next guy to score a point would be the state champion. The suspense was excruciating, and the arena was rocking.

For the second overtime, Chris started on top—not necessarily a good thing for him. For all of his strengths, he was just okay in that position. All Pierce needed to do was escape, and he'd win. With Chris riding behind him, Pierce threw his hips then twisted suddenly, turning to face Chris. Pierce very nearly won the match in that moment. But as he turned, Chris followed, barely managing to snag Pierce's left foot, which he secured in what we called the "baseball bat" grip—one hand on the shoelaces, the other on the heel. You need a solid, two-handed grip to prevent the other guy from mule-kicking his way out of it.

But Chris couldn't just hold on to the foot; he needed to work his way up Pierce's leg, or risk getting called for stalling. Slowly, painstakingly—the crowd going bananas—he stood, brought Pierce's leg up under his armpit, then took him down to the mat.

I don't know that I've ever been happier for anyone than I was for Chris when he won that title. I thought of the incredible amount of work he'd put in, dating back to those sessions in the summer. He was forever finishing a workout, then finding something else to do. That "Can't leave until we've done a workout!" effort, that extra, added, hard-earned fitness, had been his ally through two overtimes. It had won him a state championship.

I could do that, I thought. I'd been with him in that sauna, in those practices, challenging him (and getting my butt kicked), bear-crawling behind him. I had a long way to go, of course, but that didn't bother me. Look how far I'd come in a year! As the referee raised my friend's hand, I saw a path for myself. If Chris could do it, I could do it. Suddenly, I had a goal. I would be back in this arena a year from now, and not just to stand on the podium. I wanted to stand on the top step.

CHAPTER 4

Hunger

A lot of afternoons during our years together, Coach Williams could be found in the room before practice, alone on the mat "shadow wrestling"—working through a series of moves, his legs bound together with a rope. Why on earth would he tie his legs together? Well, if he was going to teach me some new takedown or tilt at practice that afternoon, he wanted to know how it felt to execute that move with just one leg.

He was the best coach I will ever have, yet he described himself as a "garbage wrestler." But he didn't mean that the way it sounds. What he meant was that he was kind of a scavenger, skilled at seeing a move, copying it, making it his own, then discarding it when it no longer served his needs. He was like a guy making the rounds of garage sales on a Saturday morning. That mind-set was one of the things that made him such a great coach. He was always on the lookout for moves and sequences that could help his guys.

On the wall above the mat were plaques of all the state champions Mesa High had produced. The sight of those tributes could be a powerful motivator during a grueling practice. Coach had built a proud tradition. One of the ways he kept it vibrant was to sit us down, pick out one of the champions on the wall, and tell us his story.

One afternoon, he told me the story of Cory Chatwin, who preceded me by five or so years at Mesa, where he was both wrestler and a national champion rock climber. Chatwin had these amazing, Popeye forearms—the result of scaling cliffs and hanging on sheer rock faces for hours at a time. To take advantage of his off-the-charts tensile strength—his amazing grip—Coach taught him a series of "tilts," or point-scoring moves, based on a hold called the "ball and chain."

That maneuver required, among other things, near-bionic grip strength, which Cory possessed. So he made the ball and chain his go-to move, and went from being a very good wrestler to a state champion. Coach told me Cory's story for a reason. As it happened, I had long arms, ideal for reaching through an opponent's legs and capturing his wrist. And my grip strength was above average, from getting around on a pair of crutches since I was small. Halfway through my sophomore year, Coach Williams decided that the ball and chain would be a major part of my repertoire.

I had a good grip, but it needed to be great. So I walked around school with a tennis ball in my pocket. When I wasn't crutching or taking notes, I'd be squeezing that ball. I bought a pair of those plastic grips, but they made my hands blister. I covered the handles with cloth, but it only helped a little. Finally, at a Big 5 Sporting Goods store near the high school, I found this device that you slipped over your arm. On top was a sort of lever that resisted when you pulled down on it. I walked around school with this contraption on my arm, trying to get a thousand reps a day. To further strengthen my grip, Coach had me hang on the rock-climbing wall in our gym first for ten minutes, then fifteen, lactic acid cooking my forearms from the inside. It got to the point where I could hang there for almost a half hour.

I learned the ball and chain during the second half of my sophomore season. I practiced hard at it, but once the match began, I'd forget, and revert to the moves I knew best—the cradles.

But I worked hard on it over the summer. When I wasn't pushing cars in the high school parking lot or being flung through the air by Freije—who, by then, was preparing for his freshman season at Arizona State—I worked on the ball and chain.

Here it is, broken down:

Working from the "top" position, I'd reach under an opponent's abdomen, using my right wrist to get control of the other guy's left wrist. If he was on his stomach on the mat, propped up on the platform of his arms, my first job was to collapse that platform, which I would accomplish by driving a shoulder into his back, at the same time pushing off my foot as if I were pushing a car over a speed bump, concentrating as many pounds per square inch as possible to smash him into the mat. After capturing the wrist, I'd snake my free arm through the opponent's legs, applying uncomfortable pressure to a highly sensitive area in the process. (There's a reason it's called the ball and chain.) Taking over the captured wrist with that free hand, I'd pull the other guy's arm between his legs, kind of like a drawstring. That action forced my opponent into an upside-down uppercase U, and opened all sorts of possibilities for scoring points.

The first thing I'd do was look for the keyhole.

Picture it: The guy is on his belly, with me behind him. I'm trying to pull his arm down, through his legs. But he's pulling back, *hard*. The harder he pulls, the more it forces his elbow to jut up into a little steeple. The area inside that triangle is the keyhole. With my free right arm, I try to thread it, reaching through and crooking my elbow under his, using his arm as my own personal handle. When I hook that elbow, it's called the keylock.

Keylock secured, I dig my elbow into his back, at the same time leaning away from him and lifting my arms up, almost as if I'm curling a dumbbell. In the process, I'm winching him from his stomach to his side to his back, and racking up near-fall points—which are awarded when you've got your opponent *almost* pinned. Life is good.

After a while, guys knew what was coming, so even if I got their wrist, they'd try desperately to deny me that elbow—the keyhole. My opponent might turn that elbow down, fighting hard the other way. If he started fighting *really* hard, I'd bide my time. I'd wait until that tension was strongest, and then release, using his energy to catapult myself in the direction he wanted to go. With my leg swinging up in the air like an inverted pendulum, I'd flip over, and put the guy on his back.

I tried to hit that move on Freije, which was tough because he was so much bigger, and he knew what was coming. But that was a good thing. Once my junior season rolled around, I was out on the mat with guys my own size, and things came easier.

WHEN I said earlier that I was hungry my junior year, I didn't just mean that I longed to improve on that sixth-place finish at states, which I did. I mean I was frickin' starving! I was a growing boy. I spent so much time wrestling and lifting that summer—me and Freije and some of the other guys worked out at least once a day—that my body *wanted* to start bulking up. But I couldn't allow it. I couldn't risk going up in weight class. My natural weight was around 113 or 114 pounds, but I was wrestling in the 103-pound class. I wrestled another six years after my junior year at Mesa, and I don't even want to think about how many weeks of my life I've spent jogging around in a rubber sauna suit (a latex getup designed to make a person sweat) or sitting in a real sauna, using a credit card or hotel room key to squeegee the perspiration off myself. (Wrestlers believe you sweat more that way.) But that was the toughest season I ever had for cutting weight.

A typical breakfast was a peanut butter Nature Valley granola bar. Lunch was two granola bars and a cup of strawberry yogurt. I'd get home after practice and my mom would serve me some broccoli or green beans and tilapia with salt and a little bit of lemon juice. It often startled my mother how fast I'd finish my dinner. That Thanksgiving, while everyone else tucked into a traditional repast, I nibbled at a quarter of a Subway sandwich. There were times, if I was right on the cusp of 103 pounds, that I'd refuse water Mom offered to me. "It's just *water*," she'd say. But the scale didn't care what it was.

For a normal dual meet, we weighed in an hour before we wrestled. That gave me time, after stepping off the scale, to wolf down my usual pre-competition snack: a bagel with peanut butter, jelly, and honey (I'd always been told that the energy from the honey gets into your muscles really quickly), followed by a vanilla PowerBar. I'd slam a bottle of Gatorade and some Pedialyte, a drink favored by new moms to rehydrate sick kids—and by a lot of wrestlers, because it replaces minerals and electrolytes we sweat out during a "cut."

Here is a general rule about wrestlers: We're grouchy going into a competition, and happy coming out of it, win or lose. Because, win or lose, we get to eat. After a match I'd give myself a day or so to "cheat"—which, in other words, means to eat like a normal teenager. That usually entailed at least one trip to In-N-Out Burger, where my standing order was a four-by-four (four patties of meat and four pieces of cheese) prepared "animal style" with mustard fried into the meat, pickles, grilled onions, lettuce, tomatoes, and extra sandwich spread. It was always a glorious mess, condiments leaking out all over the place. You need at least ten napkins for that burger. And as long as I was breaking the bank, I'd get fries and a vanilla shake.

The bill usually came due on Sunday afternoon. I'd be watching the Raiders game with my family, with a gathering sense of gloom, knowing that I had to start cutting soon. I'd pull on my black "sauna suit" and drive over to the high school. I didn't like running the track. People gave me looks, and I can't say that I blamed them: How often do you see a one-legged guy cranking out repeat miles on his crutches for an hour and a half wearing a glorified garbage bag? So I stuck to a more solitary route along the perimeter of the high school, a three-quarter-mile loop along the fence line. It was always satisfying, as I ticked off the miles, to hear sweat sloshing around in the folds of the rubber suit. Walking back to my car, I'd stop long enough to pull back the elastic and let some of the perspiration spill out. (Gross, I know—but necessary.)

Back home I'd drain the rest of the sweat in the shower, turn the suit inside out, and rinse it. The key was making sure it dried all the way. I hated putting on a sauna suit that was still damp on the inside, because the moisture got cold, which meant it took longer to start sweating the next time I put it on.

As long as I was sweating even a little after a run, I held off showering. (Again, sorry if that's too much information.) Every fraction of an ounce of sweat helped. We had one of those digital bathroom scales that didn't register your weight right away. Each time I stepped on the scale I endured this drumroll moment before the number popped up. Some nights, the number was low enough that I could justify a light snack before bedtime. But there were plenty of nights when I went to bed hungry.

That would make me a little ornery the next day, and I would take that meanness out onto the mat with me. Someone would have to pay.

I expected to be much improved as a junior. I did *not* expect to cruise through the season undefeated, rolling up fat margins of victory and just crushing opponent after opponent. The time I'd already put in with Coach Williams, the progress we made honing my style; the foundation I'd laid with those grueling off-season work-outs with Freije and the guys; and the addition to my repertoire of the ball and chain—it all added up to a dominant season.

I wrestled forty-eight matches and won 'em all. I was never scored on, never taken down, never put on my back. I did allow some opponents to escape—usually in order to keep the match going, so I could use them to brush up on my takedowns. When I'd had enough practice, Coach would give me the signal, and I'd end the match.

The one opponent that very nearly derailed me was my appetite.

IN 2005 they switched the venue of the state wrestling tournament, from downtown Phoenix to the Jobing .com Arena in Glendale. The day before the semis for the 103-pound weight class, I was up to 111. I didn't panic; I'd cut eight pounds in a day before. But on this occasion, the weight wasn't coming off. I was so tired, so burned out, that I had trouble getting a good sweat going. After spending my usual, miserable hour-plus in my sauna suit, and more time in an actual sauna, after going to bed hungry and thirsty—I usually dropped a couple pounds during the night—I woke up the day of my match and was *still* two or three pounds overweight.

UNSTOPPABLE

I headed over to the high school and got on one of the aero bikes, with Freije periodically whispering in my ear, "State champion." During the half-hour drive from Mesa up to Glendale, Coach blasted the heat in the van—which didn't especially thrill my teammates. I was in the back, wearing three sweatshirts and covered with blankets doing push-ups, sit-ups, crunches, trying to get a sweat going.

Once we got to the Arena, they lined us up by weight class. We were a salty, sullen crew. Everybody was cranky because everybody had been cutting weight. I had Freije and a handful of teammates around me so I could lean on them, and so they could hide me. I was dead tired and we didn't want the guys on the other teams to see how weak I was. When it was my turn to step on the scale, I made weight by something like five ounces. An official marked a little x on my arm, Coach Williams handed me a bottle of Gatorade, and I just started chugging it.

My strategy for the semifinals was simple: Get it over with. Because I was exhausted, I just wanted to blast my opponent in the beginning, finish him off quickly, then get some rest for that night's final—but it didn't end up working out that way. I did gradually build a substantial lead, but it took longer than I wanted it to. I bled the final minutes off the clock by stalling, running away from the guy. It wasn't pretty, but it got me to the finals.

A year after sitting in the stands, hearing the crowd's

roar during Freije's double-overtime victory, I was on the cusp of a state title of my own. Everything was working out just the way I'd pictured it. I'd envisioned this so many times, it felt almost familiar. For some reason, that failed to prevent me from being so nervous I thought I might lose my lunch.

They start the final night at the state tournament with the Parade of Champions. All the wrestlers who've advanced to the finals promenade out, then line up across from their opponents. They make a fuss over us. The announcer says, "Gentlemen, please shake hands," and then everybody runs back through the tunnel— everybody but the two guys wrestling first.

That was me and Ben Kauffman, a smart, crew-cut kid from Sandra Day O'Connor High. I'd never wrestled him before and wasn't sure what to expect. But he made me nervous. In my first-ever varsity match the previous season, a guy named Grant Cordner from Mesquite High had just wiped the mat with me. I forget the exact score—I think I must have subconsciously deleted it from my memory—but it wasn't close. It was the worst beating of my high school career. So I'd been nervously keeping an eye on Cordner, who finished the regular season with a record of 40–1. I fully expected to meet him in the finals—until Kauffman knocked him out in the qualifying round. *Wow*, I remember thinking, *this guy must be good.*

In both my first and second matches of the state

tournament, I'd pinned my opponent in sixty-four seconds. Not happening with Kauffman. Our match started slowly, as we felt each other out. Then he started coming at me with more aggression—smacking my ears, butting the top of his head into my face. I tried to stay cool on the mat, but after about the fourth time he hit me in the face, I got angry and started attacking and racking up points. I was still on the offensive with only fifteen seconds left in the final period. Later in the semester, at an awards banquet for the Mesa public schools, they showed a video of the final twenty seconds of the match. Kauffman looks like he's in pain, which makes sense because he's losing, 13–0, and because I'm on top of him, vigorously digging my elbow into his back. I'm looking at the clock with a big smile on my face, counting down the seconds until I became a state champion.

The first person I hugged, of course, was Coach Williams, who shouted in my ear over the crowd noise, "No one can take this away from you!" But there was only one guy who could have done so much to help me get it in the first place. Thanks again, Coach.

It was beyond sweet, sharing that victory with my mom and Ron, who was also in the bleachers that night. (Things were going well at home.) It was a really good night. I felt a mixture of joy and relief and, behind those emotions, a faint hunger—and not the sort of hunger that I'd take care of at In-N-Out later that night. I was already looking forward to next season.

CHAPTER 5

"Just Keep Doing What You Do"

A few days after I won state, I went on a website called AZWrestler.com. I'll admit it: I thought people might be saying nice things about me. And some were. But there was also a thread that bummed me out and made me angry. The guy who kicked off the conversation said—I'm paraphrasing, because it was a long time ago—"I couldn't help thinking that because he only has one leg, Anthony Robles has an advantage."

And it was on. The subject of my missing limb and whether or not it gives me an advantage has fueled a sort of virtual bar-stool argument ever since. A thread on Flowrestling.org asked: "Does having just one leg give Anthony Robles an unfair advantage because his opponents do not know how to wrestle somebody who is missing one leg, and in addition, the weight that would be in his leg is added muscle to his upper body?"

"The average human leg is 20 percent of the total body weight," replied one commenter. "So at 125, Robles has the rest of the body of a 156-pound wrestler . . . big advantage."

It's all very confusing to me. At different times in different places I've read that I have the upper body strength of someone wrestling at 149, 157, and 165 pounds. Later, when I faced Iowa Hawkeye Matt McDonough in the NCAAs, the number seemed to go up the closer one got to the state of Iowa. A *Sioux City Journal* columnist named Steve Allspach confidently asserted that I have "the strength and power of a 174-pounder." Do I hear 184? Anyone for 197?

There can be no doubt, Allspach concluded, "Robles wrestles with a distinct advantage."

What is sometimes overlooked, I've noticed, is the fact that it's also a mild inconvenience for me, wrestling at a high level with one leg.

I appreciated it when Jim Rome weighed in on the topic, simulating a dialogue with someone who believed I was competing with an unfair advantage:

"You mean the guy he's *wrestling* has an advantage, right?"

"No, no—the guy who's missing a leg has an advantage."

"How's that?"

"Well, because he doesn't have that [leg], he's got extra strength in his upper body."

"Yeah, right, I guess. But you do remember he's missing a leg, right?"

"Well, uh, yeah, but because he's missing a leg, there's less of him to grab."

"Okay, sure. But, one more point. HE'S MISSING A LEG! Yes, that's one less leg for the other guy to grab onto, but it's one less leg FOR HIM TO STAND ON."

Rome wasn't finished. "Wrestling is based in large part on balance, and I don't think you need to be Dan Gable to know that missing a stick is not enhancing one's balance. I mean, I can't believe I've got to take up for this guy."

AT times I let the criticism roll off my back. At other times, I've gotta be honest: It got to me and made me furious. So while I was more angry than I had been my junior season, I was, thankfully, less *hungry*.

Alleluia, I had moved up a weight class! Wrestling at 112 pounds didn't exactly give me a license to strap on a feed bag for every meal, but it did give me a *little* margin for error. It meant that, once in a while, I could put dressing on my salad. It was almost as if my body had been waiting for the signal: As soon as I bumped up to 112, my arms, chest, and shoulders started popping like a bag of microwaved popcorn. At matches, some of the other parents would see me and say nice things like, "Looks like *someone's* been working out." I had been working out all along. What was new was that I could finally eat more like a normal person.

I picked up that season where I'd left off as a junior. I had very few competitive matches. Before meets, the coaches would look at the other team's starting lineups. If the team's best wrestler was at 119 or 125, I'd take him on, rather than the guy in my own weight class. I wasn't worried so much about getting my winning streak snapped—I just wanted to get better every week. Coach Williams had been talking to me about life after high school. He felt like I had an excellent chance to wrestle in college, and at a pretty high level.

And I already knew where I wanted to wrestle.

Another of Freije's habits that I'd adopted was his post-practice custom, cranking out some miles on a stationary bike while watching a video. But not just any video. He had a cultish attachment to a documentary called *The Season: Iowa's Men of the Mat*. It was an inside look at the University of Iowa Hawkeyes' wrestling program. Better than anything I've seen before or since, it captured the stark brutality and beauty of our sport. Watching the Hawkeyes sweat and bleed and go to war worked better than a Red Bull at firing me up for that last half hour of a workout. It gave me a peek into the world of collegiate wrestling and the career that I could have in it.

I went undefeated my senior year, too. Because he believed I had a future in the sport, Coach Williams actually spearheaded a fund-raiser to get me a flight to Philadelphia for the national meet. He'd been instrumental in getting me to the national meet in Cleveland the year before, when I'd taken second place after losing in overtime in the finals. My mother was streaming the radio call of that match and wept bitter tears when I lost. She vowed then that if I made it back to Nationals my senior year, she'd be there.

I made it back to Nationals. This time they were in Pittsburgh, and I had no idea she was coming. She rented a car and showed up after my first match—but only after clearing it with Coach W. She was afraid she'd be a distraction. "Are you kidding?" he said to her. "We need all the support we can get!"

Honestly, I wasn't overflowing with confidence heading into Pittsburgh. It was one thing to be the best wrestler in my state, but this was a much bigger stage. I masked my uncertainty. I felt like I had to. I wasn't just trying to win a national title. In some ways—don't laugh—I felt like I was fighting for a better life. I was trying to break down a door, trying to get into the best college with the best wrestling program that I could. A lot of the guys at this meet had already been offered full scholarships. Not me. If any of the coaches from big-time programs were deeply interested in me, they were doing a great job keeping it a secret. I wrestled that week with a tinge of desperation. By making a big splash at Nationals, by beating the best of the best, I would be forcing their hands. That, at least, was my thinking.

In the finals, I faced an excellent wrestler named Justin Paulsen. He was very conservative and very defensive in the first period. He didn't take me down, but I couldn't take him down. Going into the second period I was nervous, because I hadn't scored. I sneaked a look at Coach Williams, who gave me a shrug, as if to say, *So what, it's close, big deal. Just keep doing what you do.*

I chose top to start the second. Usually you see wrestlers choose bottom in that situation. All you have to do is escape, and that's a point, right there. But I chose top. Leaning into Paulsen, I noticed right away that he was still breathing hard, that his lungs were burning up on him. It was like smelling blood in the water. I used a "tightwaist" hold on him, pulling his hand toward me, compressing his rib cage while digging my shoulder into his back. That series has the effect of making it difficult for the opponent to get air into his body. It worked. After doing my best to deprive Paulsen of oxygen, I attacked his wrist, got it, hit the ball and chain on him, and started piling up back points. The final score was 9–2, and I had just won my first national meet.

I was euphoric, of course, and tried to work my way up through the stands to share the triumph with my mom. Between us, however, were a handful of wrestling coaches who wanted to congratulate me—and who wondered if we might talk later. I was, and am, grateful for their interest, but I couldn't help thinking as they shook my hand and slapped me on the back that they were *the wrong coaches*! I wanted attention from the Iowas and Oklahoma States of the world, and these guys were from smaller schools in Division II and III.

Surely that would change now? The guy I'd just dominated in the national title match was headed for Stanford on a wrestling scholarship. How about me? Normally, when you win at the national meet, when you've just proven that you're the best wrestler in the country in your weight class, you get multiple scholarship offers from various name programs. But I wasn't generating much interest. Bobby Williams was hearing that college coaches were concerned about my size. The NCAA had recently done away with its 118-pound weight class, so the smallest class was now 125. Meanwhile, I was weighing in at a robust 112–113 pounds. I was going to need some seasoning, some ripening. I'd probably redshirt my first year—that is, practice with the team but not compete, thus preserving four more years of eligibility. I'd spend that first year bulking up, gaining strength, and establishing a firm academic foundation. But I could do that—plenty of guys had done that.

The truth, of course, is that wrestling is a cruel sport, and the men who coach it at the Division I level had concluded that what worked for me in high school could not work at the next level. They figured that the athletes were too quick and strong and smart. Maybe if some three-limbed pioneer had come before me, they might have mustered up the nerve to take a chance on me. But nobody was. Nobody wanted to be the guy who squandered a scholarship on the one-legged kid who didn't pan out.

Nobody except for Jack Childs, that is.

Jack was the legendary coach at Drexel University, an excellent, underrated, up-and-coming school in west Philadelphia. Childs had been at Drexel for three decades and was the winningest coach in Division I. His tough exterior failed to disguise his warmth: He was a tenured assistant professor who cared about his athletes. On my official recruiting visit to the school, he looked me in the eye and told me, "We want you to come to Drexel and be the face of this program." It was tempting. I had offers from a bunch of Division II schools and Drexel was the only D-I school that offered me a full ride.

Dating back to my first match in ninth grade, when my mother got right up in the face of that woman who'd laughed at me, she made it her business to see me wrestle as often as possible—she'd been to almost every single match. Ron made it to my matches less frequently—he usually had a day job to do—but it made me feel good when he did show up. After some heated arguments with my mom—who had accompanied me on recruiting trips to some smaller schools—we decided that Ron would join me on my trip to Philly for my official recruiting visit at Drexel.

I'm glad he did. It ended up being one of the best times we ever had together. We got picked up at the airport. Coach Childs and his staff made a fuss over us, showed us the campus and took us out on the town, always talking about how they saw me as one of the key components in rebuilding the program.

Someone told us the "*Rocky* steps" were nearby. You know, that scene in *Rocky*, at the end of Sylvester Stallone's training sequence, where he sprints up the seventy-two stone steps at the entrance of the Philadelphia Museum of Art as the music reaches a crescendo. Well, some of my best memories with my stepfather were of us watching *Rocky* together. We loved that movie. So after dinner, we set out walking. The museum was more than a mile away. I remember we walked north past a huge switching yard, then onto a bridge that took us over the Schuylkill River. We arrived long after sunset. The steps were dark, which just made the skyline of the city glow that much brighter.

We had the place to ourselves. It was the end of a long day and neither of us had much energy. And so we walked up the *Rocky* steps. I don't even remember what we talked about. But it was a huge deal for us, a great bonding moment. At the top of the steps you're facing south and east, and it feels like you're looking directly into the heart of Philadelphia. It was stunning. I had a lot of struggles with my stepfather and some huge problems with the way he treated my mother. But there were more than a few times when he was kind and generous with me. We had some really good moments. We had fun. For Ron and me, it never got better than that night at the top of the *Rocky* steps.

After our trip, he was *sold* on Drexel. In his mind, it was a slam-dunk: full scholarship, living expenses—who else was offering me that kind of money? I wasn't so certain that it was the place for me, but if I'd learned one thing growing up under his roof, it was conflict avoidance. And so I smiled and nodded and agreed with him that, yes, Drexel was awesome. But in my heart I knew it was too far from home. I knew that Arizona State, ten miles from our house, had a proud wrestling tradition. I had a good relationship with the head coach there. Thom Ortiz didn't have an athletic scholarship for me, but he invited me to walk-on to the program. If I did well, I'd have the opportunity to earn a scholarship, he told me. In the meantime, I applied for and was awarded a grant from a charity called Chicanos Por La Causa, Inc. That helped a lot, as did ASU's willingness to cover the cost of most of my books.

Mom wanted me to go to Drexel because she liked the coaches there. She appreciated that they appreciated me. She also believed that it would be healthy for me to get out of that house, to put a couple of time zones between myself and their daily drama. Ron wanted me to go to Drexel because the price was right. But as he reminded me so often, "You need to grow up. You need to go away to become a man. You can't be a mama's boy forever."

I knew there was going to be a firestorm when I broke the news to them that I was going to ASU, but that's where I knew I needed to be. Judy supported me and respected my decision. Ron was less understanding. He took it poorly. I was the one who'd put in the work, who'd shed the sweat and blood to earn these opportunities. It was my life, and my call. But my stepfather didn't see it that way. He got pissed at me, and he pretty much stayed pissed. But he wasn't just angry with me. The topic of where I would go to college became a major hot-button issue for him and my mom.

When wrestling ended after my senior season, I missed it more than usual. Not because I missed the time commitment, or the physical torments, or the privation. More and more, I was feeling the need for sanctuary. Coach Williams used to tell us that the wrestling room was a sanctuary, a place where we could check our cares at the door.

I needed a place like that because, by that time, home had stopped feeling like home; I didn't look forward to spending time under that roof as long as Ron was there. There was a pattern in our family life: brief periods of normalcy and tranquility followed by the inevitable storm. My junior year had been an unusually long period of calm, and prosperity. Ron had a good job. There was peace in the land. I'd come home from practice, say hi to my mom and my brothers and sister. Ron would be sitting in front of the TV. Maybe he'd say hi back to me, sometimes he'd just nod his head in my direction.

But now, more often than not, he was angry. One of us kids was usually getting yelled at for something—anything—so the best plan was to avoid him and stay out of his way. I'd come in and just go straight to my room, a converted carport I shared with my brother Nicholas.

At some point during my senior year, Ron hooked back up with his old girlfriend—again. And Judy found out about it—again. He'd already stepped out on her many times, but she would always take him back because she felt like she could change him. God bless her, every time she learned of one of his indiscretions ("He cheated on me sixteen times, that I know about," she says), she was shocked and surprised and hurt all over again. After a while, she stopped giving him the satisfaction of reacting when she would find out about his latest instance of infidelity. She would shut down, like a zombie, which would infuriate him all the more.

Judy had been out of work for years, raising five

kids. But it was around this time she started working part-time and taking college courses. She finally realized that things weren't going to get better with Ron, and saw her marriage for what it was—a nightmare.

The night of my high school graduation, my grandparents came in from out of town. It was a special day—a celebration—but it was also very uncomfortable. Becky and Marc were angry and upset with Ron, who they knew was cheating on their daughter once again. There was special seating up front for the families at the commencement ceremonies, and I remember that Ron and my mom sat together, even though they weren't getting along at all. It was a happy night, but it was sad at the same time.

The firestorm was on the horizon. Things were getting worse, not better. While my graduation marked the beginning of a new, exciting chapter in my life, my mother remembers that time as the beginning of the end of her marriage.

CHAPTER 6

"You're Gonna Be a Champion"

I'D been at Arizona State for a few weeks when an alumnus left an early-morning voice mail for Coach Ortiz:

> *I'm on my way to work, driving down Rural Road, thinking about how much pressure I'm under, and how tough I have it, and there's a bunch of wrestlers running on the side of the road. Then I see this kid, sprinting on his crutches at six o'clock in the morning! So I start thinking, "What am I bitching about?"*

That motorist had seen us running a mile for time. It took me ten minutes on the first try, but I got that down to eight. Coach and I butted heads over another preseason workout, the wrestling team's traditional two-mile run up Squaw Peak, a twisting, technical trail that kicks up fiercely at the end.

"Anthony," he would say, "you don't need to do that."

"Coach," I would reply, "I'm doing it." The truth was, it was dicier for me getting *down* that trail. As Thom pointed out, "You start rolling down that mountain, you're gonna be rollin' for a while."

Just as it had been in junior high, then high school, I needed to show my teammates that I was all-in, that I wasn't looking for special treatment, that I could do every workout and every drill they could do—and that, sometimes, I could do it better.

From that cramped, borrowed little sweatbox of a wrestling room at Mesa Junior High, I'd moved on up to the MHS Jackrabbits facility, which is, as high school wrestling rooms go, spacious and above average. And yet you could fit four or five of those rooms into the 9,600-square-foot Riches Wrestling Complex, the practice facility at Arizona State. Its vast surface of maroon mats featured twenty or so wrestling "circles." Nine were big, the rest were smaller. As a walk-on newbie, I was relegated to one of the smaller circles, far from the center of the room, where the best wrestlers claimed their turf. I was awestruck at first, and spent a lot of time studying the pictures on the far wall, portraits of Arizona State's past national champions.

There was Curley Culp in 1967, a heavyweight and

future NFL star who went on to play in six Pro Bowls. There was Dan St. John, who won the NCAAs at 158 pounds in 1989 and at 167 the following year. And he was a walk-on, just like me! Likewise, Markus Mollica had won two national titles, in '93 and '95. The most recent Sun Devil to win it all was 149-pounder Eric Larkin, in 2003. A total of six ASU wrestlers had won NCAA titles—I dreamed of making it seven.

However, before that could happen I would have to, you know, wrestle in an actual varsity match, which looked like it wasn't going to happen my freshman year. Coach O and his assistants took one look at me and made up their minds: I was redshirting. As I mentioned, the lowest collegiate weight class had been raised to 125 pounds and I was still bouncing around the low 110s. I needed to put on about twenty pounds of muscle in order to be a decent-sized 125-pounder. It made sense that I exercise patience, and use the extra time to my advantage. It was only logical.

Screw logic. At the Maroon and Gold match, I was scheduled to wrestle off against John Espinoza, a tough kid who had graduated from Maryville High in Phoenix. Sure, everyone on the team expected me to redshirt. But, I thought, if I beat Espinoza, maybe I could change their minds.

I was feeling good about my chances early in the first period, when I took him down with a move that was quick and slick. *These college guys aren't THAT tough.*

But in the second period, he pinned me. I hadn't been pinned in a match since ninth grade. I remember thinking, *This is gonna be harder than I thought.*

Coach O reassured me. It's very common for guys to come in and redshirt. The gap between an eighteen-year-old true freshman and a twenty-two-year-old senior is often so pronounced that it behooves most wrestlers to spend that first season gaining strength and confidence, and settling in academically. Ortiz pointed out that even the great Cael Sanderson, an Olympic gold medalist and one of the greatest amateur wrestlers the USA had ever produced, redshirted his first year at Iowa State. Thom had been an assistant coach with the Cyclones at the time.

We were at the tip of a pyramid that was getting increasingly difficult to climb. Wrestling at the high school level has never been healthier: Participation has grown by more than forty thousand over the past decade, according to the National Wrestling Coaches Association. But the story is very different in Division I. Thirty-five years ago there were 180 D-I programs. Today there are around eighty. Many of those programs fell victim to Title IX, a well-intentioned but often misapplied federal edict mandating that schools must provide as many athletic opportunities for women as men. If you've got a ninety-six-man football team that's filling the stadium and paying the bills, athletic directors have no choice but to look elsewhere to balance the equation. Too often, their gaze has fallen on the wrestling team. During the recent severe recession, budget cuts have been the reason cited for axing programs, as those of us in the ASU Sun Devils program would come to know.

The end result is more problematic: talented high school wrestlers chasing dramatically fewer scholarships. Still, I was determined to earn one, although it didn't help my cause that, according to a rumor I heard, at least one high-ranking administrator in the athletic department had doubts about whether I deserved it.

THOM Ortiz came from a tough neighborhood in south Tucson. "In the fall we played football, in the winter we wrestled, and in the spring we got in trouble," he says, with a laugh. "We didn't have a sport, so we went around being punks."

The son of a boxer, Ortiz wanted to box, "but my dad didn't want us to keep getting hit in the head. So he made us wrestle." Thom was a two-time state champ at Sunnyside High in Tucson, then wrestled for the Sun Devils during the program's glory days. From 1986–1990 he went 118–34–2. After moving down a weight class as a sophomore in 1988, he placed fourth at the NCAA Tournament, helping ASU win the only team title in school history.

Like Coach Williams, Thom wrestled under Bobby Douglas. When Douglas took the Iowa State head-coaching job in 2002, he brought Ortiz with him as an assistant. In Ames, Thom recruited then mentored the incredible Cael Sanderson, who went 159–0 as a collegian, earning four NCAA titles before winning a gold medal in Athens.

When he returned to his alma mater as head coach in 2001, Ortiz adopted as his motto "Back to the future." He wanted to restore the glory of the late '80s, when the Sun Devils won one national crown and were twice runners-up. In his second season, the team placed fifth in the country, with Larkin wining ASU's first individual NCAA title in eight years. Thom's teams won three Pac-10 titles between 2004 and 2007. But his squads weren't coming close to contending for national championships. After the 2006–07 season, he was summoned to a meeting with ASU athletic director Lisa Love and associate A.D. Don Bocchi.

"I was fired," he recalls, "but I talked to Lisa for an hour, and they let me stay on as coach."

Our first dual meet was in Davis, California. There were a lot of just so-so wrestlers I could have drawn for my first-ever college match. Instead, mine would be baptism by fire. I was going up against Marcos Orozco, a nationally ranked senior who'd placed third in the Pac-10 the previous season. I went on TheMat.com, trying to find out whatever I could about him. The message boards were not encouraging. There were comments like, "Doesn't look good for Anthony."

That was all the more reason for me to come out swinging—which is what I did. I shot his leg, got it, put him on his butt. But Orozco spun sideways, like a dervish (dude was quick!) and somehow twisted around and ended up on top of me. He got the points for the takedown. Not a good start for me. I was anxious.

Second period, my choice: Did I want to start on top, or bottom, or neutral? Again, most guys choose bottom. Escaping from the bottom position is considered an easier way to score.

But I chose top, and Orozco found out why. I attacked his wrist, got it, snaked my free arm between his legs, captured the wrist with that hand, and then went to work. Once I've got the wrist, I start executing a sequence of moves, kind of a big combo platter of holds and tilts that changes, depending on how my opponent tries to counter. I tilted Orozco three times for six quick points in the period, then held him off for a 7–5 win— my first as a collegian.

I'd been a bit of an X-factor to my coaches; they knew I worked hard in the room, and more than held my own against my teammates. Now they seemed happy for me, and more than a little surprised.

NEXT up, the Portland State Duals, in Oregon. My opponent was Trevor Lofstedt, the number-one-ranked wrestler in the NAIA. I beat him 17–1. A few days later, at home against Embry-Riddle, I beat their 125-pounder by the same score.

Piling up the points is a good thing in wrestling, because you're helping your team. Winning a decision by one to seven points earns three points for the squad. But there are ways to earn "bonus" points. A "major decision"—winning by eight points or more—is worth four for the team. A "technical fall" occurs when a wrestler goes up by fifteen; it's basically our sport's Mercy Rule. If the winner scored some back points on the way to that margin—that is, if he got the other guy's shoulder blades close to the mat for more than a few seconds; if he *almost* pinned him—the technical fall is worth five points to his team. If not, the team gets four. Wrestlers are always talking about how they "teched" an opponent or "majored" him. Now you know what they're talking about.

"Sticking" your foe—pinning him—was worth six points to your team. Midway through my first season, I was happy to not just be winning matches, but to be winning them by margins that earned bonus points for my team. On one tough road trip in January, I won matches at Cal Poly, Cal State Bakersfield, and Cal State Fullerton with a technical fall, a major decision, and a pin, in that order. To the surprise of at least one Sun Devils administrator, I was emerging as one of the more reliable point-scorers on the team.

At the Keystone Classic in Philadelphia, in a cool old auditorium called the Palestra, I made it to the semis and knocked off the top seed, a senior from Tennessee-Chattanooga named Javier Maldonado. But I got pinned in the finals. And that was the story of my first season in college: two steps forward, one back. At the Cliff Keen/Las Vegas Invitational, I opened up an 11–0 lead on my opponent . . . who proceeded to stick me. I took a kind of lazy shot at his legs; he got me in a headlock and ended the match.

But I learned from every mistake. As the season wore on, I was gaining confidence. I was becoming dangerous.

One of my favorite memories from that season was our dual meet with Oregon State. The athletic department was cash-starved, and looking for creative ways to sell a few extra tickets. So they switched venues, from our usual home of Wells Fargo Arena, to the gymnasium at . . . Mesa High! Five hundred or so fans jammed into the gym on my old stomping grounds. I was nervous, but excited to be coming home. I was 16–6 and ranked sixteenth in the country. I hadn't done anything yet, really—hadn't come close to the goals I'd set for myself. But as I sat on the team bus as we rolled down South Harris Drive, then pulled into the parking lot where Freije and me and a few other nut jobs used to push cars over speed bumps, I couldn't help thinking that the hard work had been worth it.

I must have known—and said hello to—every other

person in the gym that night. I was distracted and battling some butterflies, and my match was the first one of the night. OSU's Jake Gonzales got the best of me early. But I settled down, found my mojo, and cruised to a 15–7 win. But the Beavers ended up beating us as a team 27–14—our fourth straight loss. Afterward, Coach Ortiz pointed out to reporters that "we started eight freshmen tonight, and I feel our program is headed in the right direction." It was almost as if he was speaking directly to his superiors in the athletic department, pleading for patience from the people who'd already come *this* close to firing him.

I had a great match at Oklahoma, pinning my opponent after eighty-two seconds. As usual after a match, after shaking my opponent's hand I hopped over to then shake the hand of the opposing head coach. In this case, that was Jack Spates. I guess I made a pretty good impression on him, because he ended up visiting me at home the following spring, under circumstances I'll soon explain.

For the most part, those post-match handshakes between wrestlers are perfunctory, cold, not heartfelt. This isn't a warm, friendly sport, after all. It is, as Iowa head coach Tom Brands puts it, "a miniature battle between two people with strong wills.

"In order for my athlete to be successful, he'd better be an a_____. He'd better be a d___. He'd better be selfish, and he'd better be mean. It's you or the other guy. Win, you live. Lose, you die."

Brands shares that cruel worldview early on in the *The Season*, the documentary I basically memorized in high school. I'd cue it up on a VCR after practice, put on a couple sweatshirts over a sauna suit, jump on one of the Schwinn exercycles—the ones that worked your legs and your arms—and crank the volume. Depending on how much weight I had to cut, I'd spend the next hour or two soaking up Hawkeye lore, mainlining their intensity and attitude. ("I think wrestling's a good sport," says one of their heavyweights, "because you can break somebody. You can break their spirit; you can make them be a different person for the rest of their life.")

I'd push that left pedal with everything I had, wringing out the last ounces of sweat, keeping my heart rate high, fantasizing about wrestling for Iowa.

Of course, I never got a sniff from them, or from virtually any of the big-time programs. But while I couldn't wrestle *for* the Hawkeyes, I could wrestle *against* them. February 8, 2008, was a date I'd circled in my mental calendar as soon as I saw our schedule. That was the day Iowa came to town for a dual meet. I had trouble concentrating before the match.

Four years earlier, I'd introduced myself to ex-Hawkeye coaching legend Dan Gable and the Brands brothers, Tom and Terry, ex-Hawkeye wrestlers who'd gone on to win world championships and Olympic medals—gold for Tom, bronze for Terry, who became an assistant coach for his brother. I'd gotten their autographs that day in Vegas. Now, an hour or so before the dual, I was standing in the weigh-in line about five feet from all three of 'em. I wondered if they remembered me. I thought it best not to say anything. I didn't get the impression that Tom Brands was big on pre-match chit-chat with guys from the other team. *You better be an a____. You better be a d___.* But it was definitely a surreal moment. I'd watched these guys on TV, I'd worked to be like them, and now I'd be trying to beat them.

I was distracted during warm-ups. My eyes kept wandering to the visitors. They were wrestling royalty, and they knew it. If they carried themselves with a certain arrogance, well, they'd earned the right to swagger. They came in 16–1. They'd won seventeen NCAA titles since 1975, and would clinch number eighteen a couple months later.

They were *Iowa.* And they crushed us, 36–3. We won one bout of ten. I went up against Charlie Falck, a redshirt junior ranked third in the nation in our weight class. I was ranked fourteenth. I focused on not being intimidated by the Iowa mystique. I was wrestling the guy, I reminded myself, not the uniform. It didn't help me that the guy *in* the uniform was a returning all-American who'd won four high school state titles in Minnesota. Falck was *really* good. There was a relentlessness to him: As soon as the whistle blew, he was coming forward, coming at you, going over you, through you. That's how Iowa guys do it: They want to wear you

out, break you mentally, then do whatever they want
with you.

Falck got the first takedown and led 2–0 after a period. The word on him was that he wasn't great on bottom. To start the second I chose top, hit the ball and
chain on him, and milked it for six points. That
should've been the match. In high school that *would've*
been the match. But he came back on me in the third
period. He took me down, and I just couldn't get away.
He beat me, 8–6.

I wanted to feel good about holding my own—and
then some—against one of the best guys in the country.
I wanted to claim a moral victory for coming so close
against one of the vaunted Hawkeyes. But I couldn't. It
made me sick to have built that lead, then surrendered it.

Physically, I was a man. By this time I was benching
three hundred, knocking out fifty pull-ups in one minute, climbing the rope to the rafters with eight chains
draped over my shoulders. But in other ways I was very
much a young adolescent. My wrestling hadn't matured.
I hadn't figured out how to finish a close match. Coach
Williams had always described me as "a firecracker"—
meaning I could go off, score a bunch of points, at any
moment.

It wasn't enough to be a firecracker at this level. I
needed to develop the other aspects of my wrestling. I
needed to be smarter, to stop giving up these little positions that ended up having such a big effect on my

matches against opponents as talented and determined as I was.

Tanner Gardner was one of those guys. He was a tough, smart senior at Stanford. I took a 4–1 lead over him in the finals of the Pac-10 tournament. But *seconds* after jumping out to the lead, I let him reverse me and put me on my back for a three-point near fall. He beat me 7–6. And he wasn't done with me.

By finishing in the Top 4 at the conference meet, I'd punched my ticket for the NCAA championships in St. Louis. My reward for beating a kid from Columbia was a match with the number one guy in the country.

That was Angel Escobedo, a cagey, cat-quick sophomore from Indiana. With nothing to lose, I went on the offensive and took him down in the first minute. He returned the favor in the closing seconds of the next period, taking a 3–2 lead. In the third he flat-out shut me down, riding me out for the entire two minutes.

I was so close—Escobedo went on to win it all that weekend—yet so far. How could I let him ride me out for two straight minutes? I was big trouble in the top position. But the book on me was: weak on bottom. I needed to get that fixed.

I needed to win three matches on Friday to become an all-American. I won two. My third opponent: Tanner Gardner, who'd rallied to beat me by a point three weeks earlier, at the Pac-10 tournament. Somehow, this match was even closer. By consistently attacking *my* wrists, to prevent me from going after his—it's not for nothing Gardner was the Pac-10's wrestling scholar athlete of the year—he neutralized me and stayed out of the ball and chain.

He led 3–0 in the third, but I reversed him, then escaped to tie it up. In the waning seconds of regulation I pulled out of a headlock then shot hard, hooking his left leg and pulling it into my body. Next thing I knew, Gardner was screaming—he was afraid I was going to blow his knee out—and the ref stopped the match, on account of a "potentially dangerous hold." Coach O lost it, and I was a little upset, myself. But that's wrestling. Sometimes you've got to beat more than one guy.

In sudden death OT, we ended up rolling around in a wild scramble. When the tumbleweed stopped rolling I was on bottom, and my season was over. Gardner was an all-American, and I wasn't. It was *that* close. I lay on the mat, stunned, until Tanner reached down to help me up. A few moments later, after shaking hands with his coaches, I was hopping back to the ASU bench when Gardner stopped me and gave me a kind of shoulder hug. "You're tough," he shouted in my ear, over the crowd noise. "You're gonna be an NCAA champion."

That made me feel a little better, as did the standing ovation I received from the fans as I crutched out of the arena and into the tunnel . . . where fewer people would be able to see the tears running down my face.

CHAPTER 7

Leverage and Loyalty

MY first collegiate season was over, but that didn't mean I was finished working. Times were tough, I didn't like asking my mom for money, and I wasn't on a full athletic scholarship. That meant I was paying out of my own pocket for rent, food, and gas for my trusty '03 silver Mitsubishi Eclipse with the vanity plate that said WRESTLER, black racing rims, a big Oakland Raiders shield on the back window, and the sunroof that was usually open, so my rottweilers, Remy and Beast, could ride with their noses in the wind.

I'd worked construction, worked in the Rec Center at ASU, worked as a camp counselor. But my favorite job was cleaning planes at the Scottsdale Municipal

Airport, twenty miles north of campus. I liked being around the aircraft; it felt kind of exotic. And there was a nice variety to the job: Some nights we did a wash-n'-vac inside the jet; some nights we shampooed the carpets. And one night about a month and a half after the season ended, I was on a ladder, waxing the wing of an airplane, when I took a call from a local TV reporter. He wanted to know what I thought about the news coming out of the ASU athletic department. In response to the Arizona Board of Regents's recent decision to cut the university's budget by $26 million, Athletic Director Love had decided to ax three men's sports: swimming, tennis, and wrestling.

I told the guy I had no idea what he was talking about. Then I called one of the assistants, Brian Stith, who confirmed it for me. He told me that Love was holding a meeting in two hours to explain her decision to the athletes the university had suddenly disowned. *Yes, the decision to drop our sports had been made much earlier, but we had been spared that information for our own good.* The administrators *didn't want the bad news to distract us from our schoolwork and our sports.* That didn't go over well with me, and a lot of other people. It struck a condescending note. If they'd armed us with this information earlier, we could've started making contingency plans, right?

Later, I would get angry. But at the time, I was scared and sad and in shock. I mean, I loved Arizona

State, and had poured my heart into representing it the best way I could. And I had so much more to do! I was only getting started! *You're gonna be an NCAA champion.*

Not in Tempe, I wasn't. I called my mom and shed a few tears, and asked what I was going to do. She was upset, too. She felt angry and betrayed, but she also reassured me that I'd been put on this earth to excel at this sport, and that I'd end up wrestling again—somewhere.

That became apparent over the next few days. Arizona State released me and my teammates from our commitments, meaning we were free to accept scholarships from any other school. Of course, the last time my services had been available to Division I coaches, they hadn't exactly beaten a path to my doorstep.

This time was different. I heard from half a dozen really good schools, almost immediately. Oregon State offered me a full ride, as did Boise, American University in Washington, D.C., Cal Poly, Virginia Tech, and others. But one of the first coaches to call, and the first one to fly in and visit me and my family, was Jack Spates. He'd been at Oklahoma since 1993, transforming the Sooners from a perennial underachiever to national contender. In 2006, he was national coach of the year.

Spates sat in our living room and talked about the family environment he cultivated on the team. (The Sooners had team birthday parties—I loved that!) Like me, he is a Christian, and shared with me his faith.

I'd competed in Norman and liked the campus a lot. I'd also noticed that his wrestlers looked up to and respected him. By the end of our meeting, I was leaning hard toward Oklahoma, as were both my mother and stepfather.

But things were happening behind the scenes. Coach Ortiz, to his credit, was scrambling to save the program. He leaned on Art Martori, an ex-ASU wrestler who'd founded the Sunkist Kids Wrestling Club and was a past president of USA Wrestling. As I understand it, Mr. Martori was one of the generous benefactors who agreed to finance Sun Devils wrestling for the next three years. Before she agreed to resurrect the program, Love needed to see a business plan that detailed how the program intended to help sustain itself, going forward. When those questions were answered to her satisfaction, she rescinded her decision and brought us back online.

While this was a great victory for Coach Ortiz, it complicated his life incredibly. Remember, all of us had been given releases. We were free to wrestle anywhere. Not only was Thom going to have to recruit a new class of high school wrestlers, he was going to have to *re*-recruit his entire team.

When he called me to tell me the program had been saved, I said, "That's great, Coach. But the truth is, I'm thinking of transferring to Oklahoma anyway."

That took him by surprise. Admittedly, I was still a little hot about ASU dropping the program to begin with. Also, for a while, Coach O and the media relations people had been putting me out front, asking me to do a lot of newspaper and TV interviews. Meanwhile, I still wasn't on a full scholarship, unlike a lot of guys on the team who weren't performing at the level I was. My record, 25–11, was second best on the team. I'd led the squad in pins (four), technical falls (five), and major decision victories (seven). I'm not boasting here, I'm explaining why I felt like I deserved a scholarship, and why a bunch of other schools agreed with me.

"Don't do anything, don't sign anything," Coach Ortiz told me.

A few moments later, Stith called back. "What do we need to do to keep you here?"

"Well, OU's offering me a full ride," I replied.

The leverage those other schools gave me did the trick. Arizona State finally came through with a full scholarship for me.

In the end I went against my parents' wishes—again. I disappointed Coach Spates and stayed put. Yeah, it helped that ASU finally ponied up with a full ride. But I also felt a sense of loyalty both to the university, to Thom, and to my teammates. They weren't the ones who'd pulled the plug on the sport, but I'd be hurting them if I bailed.

I was also motivated by a pride of place. I was always hearing about how great the wrestling was in Iowa, in Pennsylvania, in the Midwest. I wanted people to know that there were some pretty darn good wrestlers coming out of my state, too.

CHAPTER 8

"I've Seen You on the News"

IT wasn't exactly a shocker that my stepdad wanted me to become an Oklahoma Sooner. He made valid points. ASU had dropped wrestling once, and I had three more years of eligibility. Who was to say they wouldn't ax the program again, this time for good?

But I always suspected that his insistence on me leaving the state was rooted in another agenda. Like a dog with a bone, he never could let go of his argument that, in order to become a man, I needed to leave home, get out of town, cut the apron strings. Until I did that, I would always be a "mama's boy."

I confess: I'm a homebody. Two years earlier, when the day arrived for me to move out of the house, my mom walked into my room. My stuff was all in boxes, and I was sitting on my bed. This is embarrassing, but I'll share it anyway: I was in tears. I was going to be living ten minutes away, but I was scared to leave home! I was homesick, and I hadn't even left yet.

She said, "Hey, you can do this." She gave me a hug, and prayed with me, and off I went. It was hard for her, too. She was going to miss having me around. But she also knew I needed to get out of that house.

Two years later, I was doing pretty well—everywhere but in the mind of my stepfather. I was voted cocaptain by my teammates, even though I was just a redshirt sophomore. Where high school had been a bit of a wasteland for me romantically, I was making up for lost time in college. I had a girlfriend I really cared about, and I was improving on the mat. I jumped out to an undefeated start, and was ranked seventh in the country in my weight class. I still loved the sport. Brutally hard as it was, wrestling never felt like a job for me. I lived for matches; I even loved practice.

One of the reasons for that was because wrestling was the one thing in my life I could control. Back at our cozy little bungalow on East Harmony Street, things were less and less harmonious.

By this time, my parents had been married for almost seventeen years. But they hadn't spent anywhere near that much time together. My stepdad had left us numerous times, informing my mother that he was moving back in with his ex, or some other woman—there were a number of them.

After a period of time ranging from a few days to a few weeks, he'd show up again, full of contrition, promising that this time he was really going to change, and we'd be a family again. And things would be okay for about a week. And then he'd start going dark again. The same guy who would bring my mom a blanket while she sat on the couch would be driving in the car with her, not long after, cursing her out, telling her how stupid and worthless she was, how she was used up.

What man would want a woman with five kids and a high school education? he'd taunt. He would actually mock her for taking him back after he cheated on her. That my mom didn't leave him sooner was a testament to how fiercely she wanted to keep our family together.

WHILE I was often the catalyst, it's not like Ron needed my help to work himself into a good rage. One night before an early-season trip in 2008, I drove to the house. If the team was going on a road trip, I liked to stop by and say my good-byes. The cars were in the driveway, but when I walked in the lights were down low in the living room, and my little brothers and sister were sitting on the couch. I heard screaming, cursing, and objects being thrown in the back of the house. My mom was crying. I heard her saying, "Don't touch me!"

I saw my sibs on the couch, scared and miserable, looking exactly the way I'd looked when I had to sit there and listen to the same shouting and screaming. And something snapped inside me. I walked over to the phone and dialed 9-1-1. I gave the dispatcher our address and told her to send someone, fast.

The cops didn't end up arresting anyone. Ron told me later I shouldn't have called the police. He made it a point to tell me that none of the other kids—none of *his* kids—would've called the cops on their own father. He never apologized for what happened that night. When he mentioned it, it was to justify his behavior. He told me the police wanted to arrest my mom, but he talked them out of it.

We had a bunch of squad cars in front of the house, lights flashing, neighbors looking out the window, stepping into the street to see what was going on. One of the officers recognized me. "Hey, I've seen you on the news," he said. "You're the wrestler." From the way he looked at me, I could tell he was embarrassed for me.

After that night, I never stopped loving my dad. I just lost respect for him.

CHAPTER 9

A Teammate, but Not a Friend

THE uncertainty surrounding ASU's wrestling program—It's dead! Scratch that, it's been resurrected!—cost us a couple of really talented guys. Brent Chriswell (184 pounds) and Todd Schavrien (133 pounds) transferred to Boise State and Missouri, respectively. Both would become all-Americans at their new schools.

But Thom brought in some talented new guys, too. The marquee newcomer was of particular interest to me. Ben Ashmore had been a four-time state champion from Dallas. At Bishop Lynch High, renowned for the excellence of its program, he was mentored by Kenny Monday, an Olympic gold medalist who'd also won an

NCAA title in 1984. After his senior year, Ben was named to USA Wrestling's all-America "Dream Team." (Yours truly was relegated to the impressive-sounding but less prestigious "Academic Team.") The most sought-after 119-pounder in the nation, he'd signed with Oklahoma State—Monday's alma mater. But things hadn't worked out for him in Stillwater. He'd transferred to Arizona State during the off-season. Coach Ortiz gave me a heads-up, telling me there was a former high school all-American coming in. Ashmore had wrestled 125 at Oklahoma State but could bump up to 133. Either way, in accordance with NCAA rules governing transfers, he wouldn't be eligible to compete for ASU this season. But he would be practicing with us.

I worked out with Ben at one of our preseason practices. We were very different wrestlers. Whereas I kind of swung for the fences on offense—I hated the idea of boring the people who were watching my matches—Ben was conservative. He preferred to keep the score low, and gave opponents very few opportunities to take points from him. He was also, I couldn't help noticing, really aggressive.

After that first workout, I told him, "Hey, I really want to work with you," but added this qualifier: "Let me know if you're gonna go up a weight class"—to 133. "If you're going to challenge me for my spot, I'd like to know." He smiled and said something noncommittal. It was really the last friendly moment we had.

With the season getting closer, we were sitting around the wrestling room one afternoon when the coaches passed around a clipboard. Each of us was supposed to write our name, and the weight class we preferred to wrestle. When the clipboard came to me, I saw that Ben had written "125" next to his name. Okay. He was gunning for me. Good to know.

I had more immediate concerns, like our upcoming roadie. After jumping out to a 2–0 start, we flew to Iowa City. I was beyond pumped. We were headed for what I considered to be the mecca of wrestling: Carver-Hawkeye Arena, home of the defending national champions.

Check it out: At three o'clock on a Friday afternoon they filled that place up with more than fifteen thousand people. The band was playing, the house was rocking. I'd never seen anything like it.

I'd tangled with Charlie Falck the previous season, back on my home turf. I'd taken a 6–2 lead on him, but couldn't close out the match. He beat me, 8–6. I'd gotten over the whole Iowa mystique thing. Now I just wanted some payback. We battled hard, and I led him, 1–0, after two periods. Even better for me, I was starting the third period on top—my strongest suit. But as I tried in vain to capture his wrist and turn him, I became suddenly aware of the crowd noise, which had reached a fever pitch. It was deafening. I started thinking, *Oh man, I don't wanna lose this one*, and I started wrestling not to lose. That's when he reversed me—came from underneath, somehow gained control of me, and was awarded two points. He beat me 2–1. I was still feeling hollowed out from that loss in Ames, two days later, when I went up against Iowa State's Tyler Clark, a stocky, muscular crew-cut dude I always found really hard to score on. He was so strong through the hips and legs that, even if I shot him and got ahold of a leg, it was hard to finish him. He whipped me, 9–3.

I was frustrated, and worried. Yeah, I cleaned up against the Embry-Riddles and Portland States of the world. But against top-notch competition, the guys I'd be fighting to place in the national tournament, I didn't do as well. At the Cliff Keen/Las Vegas Invitational, I rolled over the wrestlers from Western Wyoming and Cornell, in that order. Against a quality opponent, Minnesota's Zach Sanders, I got schooled. Conditioning was a strong suit of his, and he helped me realize that I needed to work even harder. Because he took it to me in that match. He took my best in stride, swatted it aside, and overwhelmed me, 7–3.

Shunted to the consolation bracket, I beat the next two guys I wrestled by a combined score of 36–1, and ended up placing third in the tournament. That made me feel a little better. A year earlier, I hadn't even placed.

I had a breakthrough two weeks later, at the Reno Tournament of Champions. I was the top seed in my weight class, and really wanted to make a statement.

A Teammate, but Not a Friend

I wanted to get the attention of the top guys in my weight class—wanted to let them know that, regardless of how they'd fared against me in the past, I was going to be a force to be reckoned with, come Nationals.

Not sure what got into me that weekend. I blitz-krieged my way through four straight matches—a pin, a major decision, two technical falls—and into the finals against Obenson Blanc of Oklahoma State. Blanc was a slick wrestler, a past all-American who'd taken off the previous season in an attempt to qualify for the U.S. Olympic team. He'd recently notched the one hundredth win of his college career.

I braced myself for a tough battle.

It wasn't forthcoming. I beat him 9–2, and was named the tournament's Outstanding Wrestler.

That weekend marked a turning point for me. I was over the moon, yeah. But I also felt a sense of relief, of setting down a burden. Okay, I got that out of the way. In a way, it removed a mental block. Five years earlier, a wrestler name Greg Carbajal appeared to have me solved, and my coaches worried that I might have hit some invisible ceiling. Winning my first college tournament erased the doubts I'd been having that perhaps, at the age of twenty, I'd peaked; that this distinctive style Coach Williams and I had invented had gotten me about as far as it was going to get me. Winning in Reno removed a mental block for me. *It's all good*, I thought. *My trajectory is still pointing upward.*

Until . . . it wasn't.

On December 28, my teammates and I boarded a flight to Chicago. The Midlands Championships, held at Northwestern University, is one of the toughest tournaments in the country. It's been around since 1963, which means that for nearly half a century it's been ensuring that wrestlers all over the country sit around the table watching their families tuck into Christmas dinner, while they force smiles and suck ice chips. Originally called the "West Suburban YMCA Open," Midlands has a cool tradition of being "open" to all comers, not just guys wrestling for major college programs. It's not quite so wide open anymore—nowadays you have to be invited.

After teching one guy and pinning another at Midlands, I lost 2–1 to Tyler Clark, the buzz saw from Iowa State. That was better than getting waxed 9–3—the score of our previous match, five weeks earlier. But I couldn't get any offense going on this guy to save my life; couldn't shoot his legs, couldn't get his wrist, couldn't tilt him. He reminded me of Ben Ashmore, whom, incidentally, I would now face in the loser's bracket.

Having transferred from Oklahoma State, Ashmore wouldn't be eligible for NCAA events until the following season. But he was free to compete in this independent, "all-comers" meet. So he signed up for it. At my weight class.

Ben was a teammate, not a friend. We never clicked.

Sure, I believe in the importance of team spirit, and I would describe myself as a "team guy." I mean, I'd turned down multiple scholarship offers to return to a school that had dropped wrestling, a school that had been slow to offer me a full ride. Twenty of my twenty-six wins were so lopsided that they earned bonus points for the team. But I had always felt that Ben was out there for the express purpose of taking something from me. I wasn't going to pretend I liked him, which worked out just fine, because he didn't pretend to like me. It made for an uneasy dynamic during practice. We went out of our way to avoid each other. He had his circle of training partners, I had mine. We didn't drill together, and we didn't wrestle . . . except when the coaches insisted that we square off, which they did every so often. When we did go mano a mano, he had as much success against me as I had against him. He knew my style intimately, and had answers for a lot of the things I tried.

His favorite tactic was to get me in a front headlock, or front head-cover, in which he would trap my head under his chest, squeezing my cranium while jamming a forearm into my neck, sometimes applying enough pressure to my carotid artery that I started to feel light-headed. (Thus the expression "sleeper hold.") When stuck in that hold—and I had trouble escaping from it earlier in my career—I couldn't take shots, couldn't get any offense going. Ben beat me 3–2 at Midlands.

In my final match I'd faced Ben Kjar of Utah Valley

University. He'd beaten me two years earlier. This time I beat him 17–1. So there were some things to be encouraged about. A year before, I hadn't placed at Midlands. This time I was seventh. But from where I sat, on the flight back to Phoenix, it was tough to see the bright side. I kept replaying the Ashmore match in my mind. Looking back, I can see that my wars with him, in practice and that day in Evanston, Illinois, were incredibly helpful in preparing me for the caliber of competition I would see at Nationals. Now both of us—and everyone else in the room—would know he'd beaten me. He would gain stature, and I would lose it. It was my most galling loss of the season.

CHAPTER 10

"Finish What You Started"

WHAT was *wrong* with me?

I'd been feeling kind of run-down since Midlands, but chalked it up to the normal wear and tear of the season. On the schedule at practice a few days before we left for St. Louis: a live match against my workout partner, Orlando Jimenez. He was a tough kid and a former Arizona state champ in high school, but not close to being on the level of NCAA qualifiers. But that didn't stop him from wiping the mat with my singlet on this particular day. Yeah, he wrestled 133, but still. He beat me by fifteen points. Coach O was so surprised and disappointed that he said, "Okay, you need to go again."

So we wrestled again. And Orlando destroyed me

again. It was a borderline catastrophe. The captain of the team is not supposed to get teched by his workout partner. This was not the shot of confidence I needed going into the second half of the season.

"You're done for the day," Ortiz told me. I jumped on my own special exercise bike—I'd removed the right pedal, just to sort of claim the machine as my own—and started hammering on it, hoping my sweat would help disguise my tears. I was scared, worried, and furious with myself. I was a mess. Coach came over and put an arm around me, and I'll always remember his words just then. They helped put my mind right.

"There's a lot of stuff going on in your life you have no control over," he told me. "I want you to focus on what you *can* control. And one of those things is how you're going to respond. Are you going to stay down and feel sorry for yourself? Or are you gonna rise up and say, 'This isn't going to stop me!'"

Holding me by the shoulders, he almost pleaded with me: "Don't let this blow your season. Don't give up now when you still have a chance."

I calmed down, took some deep breaths, and tried to put things in perspective. He was right; I was reacting to more than a poor practice. I was bringing outside problems into the wrestling room. For as long as I could remember, my family had been trapped in this cycle: intervals of stability and happiness followed by longer periods of marital discord and the sudden, unexplained disappearances of my stepfather. What was happening on the home front was that the good times were getting shorter, the bad times longer.

Between Ron's erratic income and tendency to wander, our family finances were in shambles. We were way behind on mortgage payments. My mother was on food stamps, and sold her blood once a week for $35. She'd make light of it, talking cheerfully about how lucky it was that she was O-positive, because the hospital needed lots of that type of blood. Our church was incredibly generous, helping us out with food, grocery money, and sometimes even a check to assist with the mortgage.

But it ate me alive to think that I was living well at college, and the people I loved were suffering, doing without. And they were. Whenever I brought up the subject of quitting wrestling in order to support them, Mom wouldn't even let me finish the sentence.

I dropped by the house one afternoon early in the season and sat with her in the kitchen. I was worried about her. She was thin and pale and distracted . . . not all there. Ron had gone to California, and Mom was feeling especially anxious and vulnerable. He'd left her for other women before but, as she put it, he'd never crossed state lines to do it. She was sleeping poorly, had no appetite, hadn't been eating. I got straight to the point. I was thinking seriously about quitting wrestling and getting a job, I told her. With Ron gone, I felt like the man of the house. I wanted to provide. It tormented me that my siblings depended on food stamps, that my mother was selling her blood to feed them. I wanted to work. I could always come back to wrestling later.

SITTING at the table, looking frail and fragile, she heard me out. She looked so weak that I was taken completely aback by the *steel* in her voice when she *emphatically* shut me down:

"No!

"You can't do it. You *can't* quit. Wrestling is what gives you *life*." Mom loved the sport, too: She never missed a home match and made great friends with the other wrestlers and parents. She saw, better than I could at the time, that this sport was taking me on a special journey. To set it aside would be to end the journey prematurely, to get off the bus before I had arrived. As she told others later, "I didn't want him stuck where I was."

"You need to do this for yourself," she told me. Then she repeated a refrain I'd been hearing from her all my life, a belief fed by the same stubborn mind-set that had convinced her, two decades earlier, not to give me up for adoption:

"You need to finish what you started."

I heard her that day and did not quit (although I would have a few more close calls before my senior season). For Mom's part, our sit-down that day flipped a switch inside her. As she would later admit, she'd been walking around like a zombie, confused, scared, disoriented. My offer to quit wrestling touched her on a deep level, penetrated the fog surrounding her; helped her snap out of it. Her marriage was a mess. Our conversation drove home for her the extent to which that mess was affecting the lives of her children. She describes that period as a kind of awakening, "the beginning of the end," when she finally made up her mind to split with Ron once and for all. It took a while, but eventually she did.

WHILE I didn't quit wrestling, I did get an unscheduled midseason holiday from the sport.

A couple weeks after Midlands, Oklahoma came to town. I was up and hand fighting with Joe Fio, the Sooner I'd dominated twice the previous season. He'd never given me any trouble. But now I couldn't take him down. I remember wondering, *Did he get a lot stronger, or did I get weaker?* I started the second period on top—had him where I wanted him!—but Fio escaped. I took him down, then he reversed me—*why was I so sluggish?*—then he pinned me. The crowd at Wells Fargo Arena was dead quiet. My coaches and teammates looked shocked. No one would make eye contact with me. Weeping with frustration, I went through the tunnel, searching for privacy. I didn't want people seeing me like this. Thom followed me, found me, and yelled, "What the heck happened out there?" Nor did he like the fact that I'd left the bench. "Get back out there with your team!" he commanded. He had a point. I was a captain and a leader. I returned to the bench.

When I woke up the next morning my throat was swollen nearly shut, and I had trouble speaking. It hurt to swallow. I went to Walgreens, bought a bottle of "instant relief" sore throat spray, unscrewed the top, and gargled with it. Nothing. I went to ASU's sports doctor the same day, and she warned me that I might have mononucleosis, a viral infection requiring weeks of bed rest. I reported all this to Coach Ortiz, whose optimistic response was: "It's a sore throat. You'll be fine."

It was, in fact, an advanced case of mono. My season was now in jeopardy.

The doctors made me lie in bed for about two weeks. I kept taking blood tests, to see if my white blood cell count, which had been drastically elevated, was back in normal range. Finally, after a few weeks—it felt like they wanted to wait until I'd lost every shred of fitness— the doctors let me return to practice, although my workload was embarrassingly light. The first few days I would do three or four of the drills with the team, and that was it. It was another week before I was able to do a complete practice. I was cutting it close. The Pac-10 championships were right around the corner. I needed to finish in the top four, or miss out on Nationals.

I was a superactive, happy kid. I only got self-conscious about my missing leg around middle school.

Moments after beating Justin Paulsen to become a high school national champion. The scholarship offers did not exactly come flooding in for me.

Warming up with Coach Brian Stith before my final match at the 2011 NCAA championships. I had butterflies, big-time.

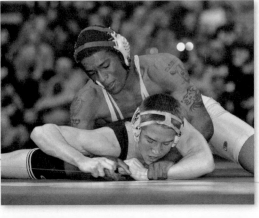

NCAA title match with Iowa's Matt McDonough. I've got his wrist, which means I'm smiling on the inside.

I like this picture my mom took of the Jumbotron at Philly's Wells Fargo Arena. I'm on the victory stand at the NCAA championships.

Celebrating with Coach Shawn Charles, who probably had to get that suit dry-cleaned. It was a long, tough journey to this moment—and worth every step.

Great day to be a Sun Devil! Bubba Jenkins and I flash the ASU "pitchfork" at Nationals. Bubba's win at 157 pounds gave Arizona State two national champions at the tournament.

The 2011 ESPYs, where I won the Jimmy V Perseverance Award. It was one of the best nights of my life.

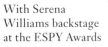

With Serena Williams backstage at the ESPY Awards

It meant so much having my entire family there with me at the ESPYs. (*From left to right:* Joshua, Nicholas, me, Mom, Andrew, and Ronnie)

Jay Leno and I hit it off when he introduced me at the ESPYs, and less than a week later he had me as a guest on his show.

How cool was it that I sat right next to Daniel Craig, who was also a guest on the show that night.

It was a kick sharing my message with the Oakland Raiders, then getting a standing ovation at midfield during the game. Most important: We beat the Bears, 25–20.

The family with former Raiders head coach Hue Jackson, who we really like and respect

Buffalo Bills (and ex-Raider) linebacker Kirk Morrison and me at the ESPYs

With Mom at the Anthony Robles Golf Invitational, a fund-raiser for Arizona State wrestling

So much has changed since I won Nationals in 2011. I now serve as an analyst on ESPN.

But one of my most rewarding new roles is that of coaching my little brother, Andrew, who is becoming an awesome wrestler in his own right.

I looked fine. If anything, I was a little underweight. The problem was, mono had robbed me of a lot of the baseline fitness I'd built up from August through December. I was still working to get that back. Until I did, I was gonna have to go out on the mat and fake it.

MY first match back was a dual meet against Stanford. I pinned their 125-pounder Austin Quarles in 2:20. The idea was to get the match over with before anyone noticed that I was breathing harder than I should have been. In a way, the Pac-10 tournament was a perfect stepping-stone to Nationals for me: It helped me figure out how to win without being in tip-top shape.

The solution: Get off the van swinging, so to speak, to hit the other guy in the mouth before he knew what happened to him. It took me just over seven minutes of mat time to win my first two matches at the Pac-10s. In the semis, I pinned Oregon State's Gonzales early in the second. In the finals, I dispatched Bakersfield's Brandon Zoeteway, 17–1. Having won the conference, I was voted the tournament's most outstanding wrestler, but I had no illusions. My record to that point was 22–6. But the opponents I'd lost to—Falck of Iowa, Clark of Iowa State, Sanders of Minnesota—were going to be the guys I'd be seeing in St. Louis. And that was if I even *went* to St. Louis. Between my mono and the latest drama with my stepfather, I'd begun to seriously question my purpose. In the days between the Pac-10 tournament and the national meet, I came extremely close to quitting the team.

RON had bailed again and headed to California. "I just need some space," he told my mother. "Things aren't working out between us." Really, Dad? Ya think?

The sadness and hardship and anger coming out of that household was so profound that it followed me into the sanctuary. I couldn't keep the mess of my personal life from seeping into the wrestling room. My motivation suffered. I was struggling to justify devoting so much of my time to a selfish pursuit when my mother needed help just to feed my brothers and sister.

Al Fuentes talked me off the ledge. Al had been a wrestler and pole vaulter at the University of Findlay, in Ohio. But he'd always felt that he'd been capable of more, and gravitated toward the field of mental coaching for athletes. After working with him in 2006–'07, Coach Ortiz had made Fuentes a full-time assistant the following season. Fuentes was really big on "using the body to regulate the mind," as he put it; using breathing and relaxation techniques to "rewire the brain" and regulate "how emotions fire." I just know that when I did what he told me, I felt calmed and centered. I wrestled better and made better decisions outside the room. He was also just a really good sounding board and mentor.

When my stepdad checked out that time, and I felt like quitting the team, I spent at least an hour in Al's office. There were times when I got so angry with Ron, when I resented what he was doing so much, that it was debilitating.

Even then, Al could see where I was headed. He saw my path clearly before I did. Earlier in the season, he'd asked me what I wanted to do after college. I told him I wanted to motivate people—I wanted to be a speaker, maybe go into broadcasting. On his advice, I switched my major from business finance to business communications. He told me I'd make a pretty good motivational speaker.

Al made me realize fairly quickly that quitting wrestling would not be a step forward. The sport was my greatest form of expression—"What God made you to do" is how my mom often put it. Throwing it overboard just to pick up a few hours of part-time work wouldn't really be helping anyone in the long run.

Al helped me to see my stepfather in a different light.

"What if one of my younger brothers played baseball?" he asked. "And what if he was poorly coached, by some guy who meant well but didn't know anything about baseball, but was filling in because no one else would?

"And what if," Al continued, "that brother went to college, and through some unlikely set of circumstances, because the baseball team was desperate for bodies, my brother was asked to join the team? So he gets thrown into the lineup, and he's horrible. Does that make him a bad kid?

"No. He didn't have a good coach, and he doesn't have talent. That doesn't make him a bad person.

"Now look at your stepfather. He was kind of thrown into fatherhood at a young age, and he's just not very talented at it. Does that make him a bad person?"

None of Al's questions changed anything that Ron had done. But they helped me see him in a different light. I found some compassion for him. I still had anger for him, but it had somehow become more manageable. It was under control. Now Al advised me to focus on the one part of my life I could control—my game. True, my family life affected my life on the mat, but it was time for me to put that aside as best I could. It was time for me to go out there and *scrap*.

I needed some of Al's calming, centering breathing exercises after getting a look at my bracket at the NCAAs. My ranking had slipped, on account of the mono. I was twelfth seed at the tournament. The lower your seed, the tougher it is to get to finals. I was looking at a meat grinder of a draw. If I won my first match, I'd be seeing a familiar face in the second.

I won my first match. At Nationals, everyone is tough, and Ohio State's Nikko Triggas was no exception. I could only pull two points out of him until late in the third period, when I escaped, then took him down for three more points. That 5–0 win earned me a date with an old friend, another guy who had my number: Iowa's Charlie Falck.

I was still trying to conceal my lack of fitness. The mono had left me weaker than usual. But as a result, it forced me to be truer to my identity than I otherwise might have been. I was the firecracker, the guy who hated to bore the crowd, who loved to rack up points. Well, this time I really needed to rack them up early, knowing I was likely to wear down in the third period. I was like a cornered, wounded animal. Before my matches at that tournament, I was much more emotional than usual. Listening to my pre-match playlist—which included some hip-hop, and always "Simple Man" by Lynyrd Skynyrd, which spoke directly to me—my eyes would well up with tears. Then I'd go out on the mat and let it all out.

I just remember wrestling like I was on fire. I felt no pressure, had no fear. My mind-set was *I'm going to run through every single person they put in front of me. I'm gonna rip everybody's head off.*

I ambushed Falck, got an early takedown, then turned him on his back for three near-fall points and a quick 5–0 lead. I tried to ride him out to end the period but he was too quick, and reversed me to end the period. Charlie chose neutral to start the second, and I knifed in for a takedown to make the score 7–2. The final score was 8–3, and after the ref raised my hand, I hopped over to Iowa head coach Tom Brands. I'd spent three years in high school listening to and memorizing this guy's Darwinian wisdom from *The Season*.

It's not that he deserves it. He doesn't deserve anything. The only thing you deserve is what you earn. It felt good to shake Coach Brands's hand as the victor, for once.

The going just got tougher. Where Falck was seeded fifth, my next foe, Northwestern's Brandon Precin, was number four. He'd won the whole thing at Midlands, and his only three losses that season had come by one point, to previous NCAA champs Escobedo and Paul Donahoe.

But after a scoreless first period, he chose bottom to start the second. I tried not to smile. He struggled to stand, but I dragged him down to the mat and hit him with three consecutive tilts, racking up nine back points and putting the match away.

That night I lost to Donahoe, the number one seed. He'd won the NCAA title for Nebraska two years earlier, then transferred to Edinboro in Pennsylvania. We were tied 1–1 in the third, he took me down to go up

3–1, I escaped to make it 3–2. With time ticking down, we ended up in a wild scramble, like a cat and dog fighting in a cartoon. I hesitated for a millisecond, and gave him just that smidgen of extra leverage he needed to score the takedown. If I had gotten that takedown, I would have won, 4–3. He got it and won, 5–2.

I have been known to get emotional after big wins and losses, but I wasn't shattered by that result. I didn't cry or marinate in self-pity; I didn't feel cheated. I felt . . . educated. "He didn't beat me because I was born with one leg," I told reporters afterward. "He beat me because he was just the better wrestler tonight."

I finished fourth in the tournament, fourth in the country. My friend and fellow Sun Devil Chris Drouin, wrestling at 141, placed sixth. But the fact that he'd produced two all-Americans was not enough to save Thom Ortiz's job. Two years after firing and rehiring him in the same meeting, a year after pulling the plug on his program, then forcing him to re-recruit all his wrestlers, Lisa Love and Don Bocchi decided to cut Thom loose. With him went Al Fuentes. I would miss them both in equal measure.

My stepdad still wasn't home by the time I got back from St. Louis. I remember thinking, *I wonder if he even knows that I placed?*

CHAPTER 11

Hell Week

THOM was replaced by Shawn Charles, a short, be-spectacled, intense, intelligent ex-wrestler who was coming home. He'd been a four-time all-American for the Sun Devils in the early '90s—wrestling at my weight class. I had heard good things about him. Like Coach O before him, Shawn talked about his desire to restore the program to its former glory. Our failure to attain those heights, in his opinion, was at least partly the result of our failure to work hard enough. And so, he introduced the team to something called Hell Week.

Let me tell you about Hell Week. Before we did any actual wrestling in the preseason, Coach Charles and his staff put us through seven days of torture designed, more than anything, to cull the herd.

The wrestling program only has ten scholarships to offer, one for each weight class. Our coaches cap the roster at thirty guys. But in the preseason, we'd have fifty or sixty people trying out for the team. Hell Week honed our conditioning to a razor's edge and built team unity, because it was an ordeal we survived together. But it also served a more utilitarian purpose: It made people quit.

We'd start a typical day at 5:30 A.M., with a six-mile run, then report to the track for a series of special torments called plate workouts. The coaches came up with five or six different lifts for us to do with forty-five-pound plates—roughly the size and shape of manhole covers. It'd be 110–115 degrees outside. We'd do nine sets, then sprint a lap around the track. Eight sets, sprint a lap, and continue all the way down to four sets. What made it *really* stink was that, by the time you finished your lap, the plate was broiling hot from sitting in the sun. My hands blistered—some guys' hands bled. There were guys off to the side, puking; guys just lying on the field, unable to go on. A lot of guys don't make it through Hell Week.

For another plate workout, they'd divide us into teams of three. We'd have to run a mile with the plate. When one wrestler got tired, he handed the plate to a teammate. When it came my turn to lug the plate,

I would slip my T-shirt through the hole in the middle, tie the ends together, and use that shirt as a kind of sling. It was brutally hard, but we got it done.

The first day we had to run six miles, Coach Charles told me, "Anthony, you don't have to do this." I let him know that I did everything that everyone else on the team did: the six-miler, the four-hundred-meter sprints, the plate relay. My feeling was—and is—"This is who I am, and I can do everything everybody else can do. Some things, I can do better." I needed my teammates to know I was going to work as hard as they were, if not harder.

"From that point on," Charles told a reporter, "I never thought about asking him if he could do a certain drill or run or exercise. Whether we were doing firemen carries or lugging plates around the track, he'd just figure out a way."

Because my teammates knew I didn't want their help, they seldom offered. When we traveled, I'd be schlepping my own luggage, while people passing by would be looking at my teammates as if to say, *Why aren't you helping this guy?*

As Charles puts it, "Because he doesn't WANT our help. YOU try carrying his suitcase for him." While I am usually adamant about getting no special treatment, there is a place where I've been known to take advantage of what Shawn refers to as my "uniqueness": to get in the express line to clear airport security.

Sorry if that disillusions you. My feeling is, if I stand in the longer line, the terrorists win.

WITH Hell Week finally over my junior year, the coaches posted a list of who had made the team, and what weight class they'd been assigned. It ticked me off to see Ben Ashmore listed at 125 pounds—*my* weight class. Ben, you may recall, had sat out the previous season, in accordance with NCAA bylaws, having transferred from Oklahoma State the year before.

The new staff's decision to open *my* weight class—and that is very much how I thought of it—to competition rubbed me the wrong way. I felt like I had earned that spot. After ASU had dropped the sport, only to restore it ten days later, I'd stuck around, despite some tempting offers to wrestle elsewhere. I was the team's leading point scorer, a returning all-American in my second season as captain. And now these guys were gonna give Ashmore every chance to take my spot? Sorry, there are some things you don't share. It felt like some other guy had asked my girlfriend out. Let Ben bump up to 133. This was my turf.

In retrospect, I realize I was out of sorts and out of line. Of course I should have to earn the position all over again. I'm just telling you how I felt at the time. I felt wounded, betrayed.

Coach Charles was unmoved. Part of turning over

a new leaf, he said, was opening all positions to competition. That's what he said. What I *heard* was that regardless of what I'd already sacrificed and accomplished, I still hadn't earned my place on the team. It felt like they were telling me that they didn't believe in me.

With the benefit of hindsight, I see that Coach Charles was being as fair as he could, and that he had the best interests of the team in mind. He knew Ben and I would push each other, just as he knew that the winner could bump up a weight class, to 133, and still win a lot of dual meets. It was a win-win for the squad. But I still saw it as a slight. I think in my subconscious, I'm the kind of guy who sometimes goes *looking* for slights. Because the truth is, I wrestled better when I had a chip on my shoulder.

Ben and I were teammates in name only. By this time I'd upgraded to one of the bigger circles toward the center of the room. Ben was against the far wall, in a smaller circle. We didn't drill together and barely acknowledged each other. But the new coaches, like the old coaches, occasionally made us go live against each other. I wouldn't say Ben had my number, but he definitely had a keen awareness of my strengths and weaknesses. And now he stood between me and the starting spot I would have to earn all over again.

It would all come down to the Maroon and Gold dual meet, our intra-squad competition on the eve of the season. In the weeks before that meet, when the coaches made us live-wrestle in practice, I deliberately kept it conservative. I didn't want to show him much. I'd dust off moves that weren't usually part of my attack, and that I had no intention of using against him when it mattered.

The wrestle-off is a peculiar animal. Coaches preach teamwork, team spirit, team building. But the wrestle-off exposes another aspect. Pitting teammate against teammate, it reminds us that our sport, at its core, is an individual one. Whereas our coaches would normally pour their hearts into the task of helping us prepare for an upcoming opponent, the wrestle-off puts them in a bind: They don't want to be seen as favoring one wrestler over another.

As a result, we were kind of on our own, preparing for the Maroon and Gold meet. Recall that Ben had been coached in high school by Kenny Monday, a former NCAA champion and Olympic gold medalist—one of the greatest American wrestlers ever. That worried me. But I was getting a little outside help myself.

I never fell out of touch with Bobby Williams, my coach at Mesa High. I had a biological father and a stepfather, but I often find myself describing Bobby as "a father figure."

A month or so before the season started, I gave him a call and told him about the tough wrestle-off I was facing. He could hear the anxiety in my voice, and asked me what problems Ashmore posed. After I told him, he invited me to come by the room sometime, "and we'll have a look." Just knowing Coach was on the case helped me relax a little.

A couple times a week, after practices at ASU and if I wasn't working, I'd hop in the Mitsubishi and make the eight-mile drive to Mesa High, then crutch over to the old, familiar room. It was always good to see Coach Williams again. As it happened, he'd made it his business to look at some video of Ben wrestling, and had some ideas on how I might fare better against him.

Ben Ashmore was one of the strongest guys I've ever wrestled. At 5'5", he was on the short side, and was one of the few opponents I ever faced who dropped down as low, or lower, than me. What he liked to do was lunge for my head, get my head under his armpit, and jam his forearm under my throat. He'd squeeze my head the way a running back squeezes the football. Once I got stuck in that position I couldn't get out, couldn't shoot. The match was no longer in my control.

That hold is called the front headlock, or front head-cover, and it had given me plenty of trouble in my college career. By dropping to a knee and staying low, I took from my opponents the opportunity to shoot for my leg. What I gave them in return, however, was easier access to my head. It hadn't been much of a problem in high school, where I was stronger and quicker than most of the competition. College was a different story. The best guys I faced—Gardner at Stanford, Iowa State's Clark, Escobedo at Indiana, Donahoe at Edinboro, and yes, Ben—were often able to get a hand on the back of my neck, yank it straight down, then cover up my head, and attack from there.

Making the hold uncomfortable is the fact that the other guy is pressing his forearm into your neck with all the strength he can muster. If that cuts off a lot of the blood flow to your brain, well, that's an added bonus for him.

Coach Williams taught me to reach up and grab the arm digging into my neck, as high as the elbow, if possible. In one sudden movement, you jerk down on that arm while at the same time spinning out of the hold. The move, called an arm drag, is pretty basic. But I'd never really mastered it. Working with Coach and a few of the high school guys who hung around after practice, I took this time to improve it, make it part of my arsenal. It would come in handy later.

Ever since high school I'd been known for my strength in the top starting position. My opponent is on all fours; I'm behind him, an arm around his waist, opposite hand on his closest elbow. I liked to think of the guy below me as a table. Digging a shoulder into his back, I would set about snapping the "legs" off the table. Then I'd attack a wrist, and try to work the ol' ball and chain.

I was far less dangerous starting down. Coach

Williams wanted to remedy that. "We need to make you more dangerous on bottom," he said.

Ben was *really* aggressive on top, pushing me down, mashing my face into the mat. But, as Coach reminded me, if the top man drove his opponent down and forward with too much abandon, there was an effective counter. I could use my grip strength to lock up the wrist of the arm around my waist, at the same time executing a quick sideways roll, throwing my hips hard, spinning until the top man found himself beneath me. That move is known as a Fat Man Roll—not sure why—and I was happy to have it in my bag of tricks going into the Friday night before Halloween.

The Maroon and Gold dual had an informal vibe that tended to disguise how much was at stake for a lot of guys. It was held right there in the wrestling room, with a few rows of folding chairs set up for friends and family, who crowded right up to the edge of the mat.

My match with Ben was first, and he took it to me early, scoring a takedown in the first period to jump to a 2–0 lead. Ben was quite comfortable in that gray area between very aggressive and dirty. If he wanted to smack your head, it wasn't going to be a love tap. He'd be swinging to take your head off. Early in the first period, we were hand-fighting when he lunged forward and head-butted me in the eye, then got a takedown. Maybe it was an accident, I don't know. But I was a little bit stunned and asked for a timeout to recover.

Going into the second period, with Ben up 2–0, I saw him look to his father, who advised him to start the second period down. They knew my reputation for being strong on top. They were trying to get into my head, attacking my strength. It was a nice piece of gamesmanship.

But it didn't work. I tilted Ben to tie the score; he escaped late in the period to take a 3–2 lead. I was 120 seconds from having to find myself another weight class. Early in the third he was on top, driving me forward, trying to smash my face in the mat, when I grabbed an arm and rolled in the direction he was going—only faster. The Fat Man Roll worked to perfection: I even hooked his knee with my free hand, used it almost like a handle while I pressed his back to the mat. The ref awarded me two points for a reversal, plus a pair of back points. The final score was 7–4. I accepted congratulations from my coaches, then walked over to say thanks to the best wrestling coach in the room: Bobby Williams.

BEN bumped up to 133, and had a really good season, qualifying for the national tournament. I started strong, too, rolling through November undefeated. My first loss came at the prestigious Las Vegas Invitational. After winning five straight matches, I ran into Indiana's Angel Escobedo, the Indiana Hoosier who'd beaten me in a close match at the 2008 NCAAs, on his way to a national title. Two years later, he was still wrestling on a different level than me. The thing that struck me about Angel was how calm and composed he stayed throughout the match. I was used to jumping out to big leads, but when I found myself in close, tight matches, I didn't always keep my composure. I let the pressure get to me. Sometimes I panicked.

Angel beat me in Vegas, 4–2. I remember sitting in the tunnel afterward, doing a kind of postmortem on the match with Coach Charles. "Do you feel like you wrestled your best?" he asked me. He knew the answer. I had cracked under the pressure. I'd been too conservative. I'd wrestled not to lose, meaning I'd been so busy preserving and defending my lead at all costs that I forgot to *pad* it. And then it was gone.

I was undefeated in dual meets, but that streak was in Intensive Care on February 7. With Iowa State in town, I drew a baby-faced assassin named Andrew Long. He was ranked fifth in the country; I was ranked third. But not for long, it seemed. My modus operandi was to come out aggressive, on the offensive, to build a lead and then drain the clock. On this particular night, in front of a home crowd that got quieter and quieter, Long was kicking my butt.

I remember glancing at the Arizona State bench late in the second period, trailing 10–2. I was in a head-lock, struggling to breathe, wondering how much longer Long could twist my left arm before he dislocated my elbow. I was *this* close to getting pinned. As I'm fighting for my life, I'm looking upside down at my teammates. Here I am, their captain, getting *worked*— and they were shocked, confused, and discouraged. I remember the look on Brian Snyder's face. He was one of our assistant coaches, and never very good at hiding his emotions. His head was hanging down, his body language saying, *Okay, let's just get it over with.*

Somehow, I made it to the end of the period without getting pinned. I'd never heard the home crowd at Wells Fargo Arena so quiet during one of my matches. On the bench, no one looked me in the eye. I was two minutes from one of the worst beatings of my career.

And then Andrew Long gave me a gift. I started the period on top. He tried to escape with a stand-up move—exploding backward into me, driving up. I had to resist the urge to thank him. I love it when guys try that. Then, just as I hoped he would, Long tried to pry my hand off his waist. I lived for moments like those. I locked onto his wrist—that was a bad thing for Long, and he knew it.

I quickly tilted him for a couple of near-fall points, bringing a smattering of polite applause. I threw the second move in combination: two more points. Now the score's 10–7 and the crowd was getting into it.

My wrists and fingers are scarred from where guys have tried to peel and scratch my fingers off their wrists.

But once I latch on, I'm not letting go. Once I've got your wrist, I've got a mental list of three or four moves I'm going to hit you with, in a row. Once I start throwing those combinations, the other guy is just along for the ride—it feels like I am in one of those Riverdance troupes, and my opponent is the ribbon I am twirling over my head.

Now I was in a rhythm, and Long was in trouble: I turned him twice more. Coach Charles was out of his chair and shouting like a crazy man, "He's BROKE. He's TIRED! You gotta WANT IT!" With half a minute left I led 12–10, so I just held him down the rest of the way, until I had heard the whistle.

"He's real tough on top," Long said afterward. "He's got an amazing grip, and these turns you don't feel coming."

For my comeback, the ASU athletic department made me the school's Athlete of the Week. It was the third time that season I'd won the award, but I wasn't about to get a big head. My night job kept me humble. After practice I'd get some dinner, never as much as I wanted, then head over to the student rec center, where I folded towels, rented out equipment, and tried to get a little homework done. I was dog tired but needed that paycheck. My athletic scholarship covered food, rent, and books, but I had zero extra money, and I wasn't about to ask my mom for any.

ALL the drama in my family was hurting my wrestling. You just couldn't tell from looking at my record. I won fourteen straight matches, cruising to my second Pac-10 title in two years. Next up: the Qwest Center in Omaha, Nebraska, for the NCAA championships. I'd finished fourth in the nation the previous season, coming off the bout of mono. I was a year stronger and smarter. I expected to improve on that performance.

I routed my first two opponents by a combined score of 32–0, and felt pretty good about my chances in the quarterfinals. My opponent: Andrew Long from Iowa State, the guy who had me upside down and in distress in front of my team the previous February—before I started spinning him like a top in the third period.

He was ready for me this time. He'd learned from his mistake. This time he kept my hands off his wrists. I had a much tougher time turning him. Still, I was up 3–2 with just a half-minute left to wrestle when we went out of bounds, and the referee stopped the match. Hopping back to the center of the mat, I remember thinking how drained I felt, how spent. I felt like I didn't have anything left. I panicked a little, and took a bad shot, kind of a halfhearted lunge at his legs. Long made me pay for it, and turned it into a takedown. For the last twenty seconds of the match he just held me down, while a nearby cluster of cardinal and gold fans just started going *off*. Long was going to the semis. I was going to the consolation round.

I could barely speak; I was so disappointed. Walking back into the tunnel, Coach Charles kept asking me if I was okay. It felt a little like I was in shock. A lot of guys don't get a chance to get to the Nationals. I'd gotten my chance, and I'd blown it. This was supposed to be my year, and I'd screwed up. I did the thing I couldn't do. I took a bad shot, and he made me pay for it. I got away from my strengths, my identity. I allowed doubt to creep in. I'd broken myself! A moment after coach asked me if I was okay, my eyes got wide and I just started bawling. Ecclesiastes tells us there is "a time to weep," and I did—hiding behind a curtain under the bleachers.

It took me an hour to regain my composure and go talk to my family. My mother and all four of my sibs had made the trip. I wanted so much to make them proud. For them to see me lose like that, and then break down—it made me feel ashamed. I hugged everybody real quick, trying not to cry in front of my mother, then headed back to the hotel room. I had another match to wrestle that day.

Four hours later I took on Michael Martinez of Wyoming, in a match that would determine whether I would be an all-American. Honestly, I didn't care anymore. Sitting in the hotel room, I felt numb. I just wanted to be done. When I got back to the arena, I didn't really warm up properly—I was still sulking. Martinez did me a favor when he fish-hooked me in the second period, digging his fingers into my cheek while I was trying to take him down. That pissed me off, and snapped me out of the funk I was in. I ended up taking out a lot of my anger and disappointment on him. I mauled him 10–1.

Before the final match—Long ended up losing to a terrific freshman from Iowa named Matt McDonough—I took part in the Parade of Champions, a ceremony honoring the all-Americans. The top eight wrestlers in each weight class marched out and stood in a straight line. "Ladies and gentlemen," the announcer intoned, "*your* 2010 all-Americans!" We turned three times, each time facing a different part of the audience. After that they played the national anthem. Then, with the crowd sufficiently amped, the two guys who made the final wrestled for the title.

That national anthem moment was one that I allowed myself to think about sometimes during Hell Week, between drills in the wrestling room, or cutting weight in the sauna. I'd envisioned singing along, then winning the big one. I'd had that opportunity in my grasp, and let it slip away, which is why I spent the entire anthem blinking back tears. The Parade of Champions felt like a Walk of Shame for me.

It was interesting to see how some people treated me differently, after I crashed and burned. A couple reporters who'd asked to meet with me afterward never did get in touch. Some of the people who'd sung my praises before were reluctant to make eye contact. It made me feel like I was old news, a loser. I made it a point to remember how that felt.

I ended up placing seventh at Nationals. Arizona State made a big fuss: For the second straight season I was an all-American. And the sky was the limit for next season, people kept telling me. What I didn't tell them was that there probably wasn't going to be a next season.

I was physically and emotionally spent. Between the rigors of the season and the emotional roller coaster my stepdad put our entire family on—looming foreclosure, my mom's struggle just to feed my brothers and sister—I honestly wanted nothing more than to go home and curl up in a ball . . . after eating a steak dinner complete with mashed potatoes heavy on the *butter*, followed by apple pie with at least two scoops of vanilla ice cream.

Two weeks later, Coach Charles called to let me know he wanted to see me back in the wrestling room. It was time to start preparing for next season. I was feeling a little burned out, and needed a break, I explained. He didn't like hearing that, but told me it was okay.

I told Coach I'd see him in a couple weeks, but in my mind, I was finished. I'd wrestled my last match. I knew how much time and sweat and suffering it would take to get back to the razor's edge of competitive sharpness where I wanted to be—where I needed to be, if I was going to get back to the NCAA tournament. The very idea of it exhausted me. I was too tapped out to make that commitment. I was on schedule to graduate in December. After that, I'd move on with my life. No more blistering my hands on broiling plates during Hell Week, no more mind games with Ben Ashmore, no more going to bed hungry, or using a credit card to squeegee the sweat off my body in the sauna. I was tapped out, physically and emotionally. I was moving on. I was stoppable.

But one day, I dropped by the wrestling offices and picked up a packet of letters from a class of third graders in Atlanta. Each student's assignment was to write a letter to his or her "hero." After reading an article about me in *Wrestling USA* magazine, they'd chosen me as their hero. All of a sudden, I wasn't so sure about walking away from the sport.

THE letters melted me. In the past, I'd had mixed feelings about this kind of attention. I suspected that people were praising me because I was the kid with one leg. I got a little more comfortable with publicity once I started winning a lot of matches in college, but I also viewed it as something that made my job harder. If people wrote me or told me I inspired them, or that they were looking up to me, their expectations became a burden. It made me feel like I *had* to win, and that if I didn't I'd be letting them down.

A lot of the kids offered encouragement, if I lost. It didn't feel like pressure; it felt like support. We were helping each other. I was drawing inspiration from *them*. It was a two-way street. I realized that, by quitting, I wouldn't be holding up my end of the bargain. Thank you, third graders, for getting me out of my own head, and reminding me that I wasn't wrestling just for myself. I was raised to believe God made me for a purpose. That purpose, it seemed, was to give people hope, to remind them that, with hard work and persistence, anything is possible.

I didn't make a decision that day. The clouds did not part. I did not have an epiphany. I simply realized, leafing through those letters at my dining room table, that it was going to be harder to quit this sport than I thought.

CHAPTER 12

Decision Time

EVEN when I was flailing around on the mat as a freshman in high school, getting pinned every other match, I loved this sport to my core. Yeah, some practices sucked, and sure, there were times in the dead of winter when I wished the end of the season would hurry up and get here. But nothing had ever come close to snuffing out my passion for wrestling.

In the days and weeks after I lost at Nationals, I lost that passion. For the first time in my life, wrestling felt like a job.

I'd finished fourth in the country as a sophomore, and expected to do better as a junior. To regress, as I had, was deeply discouraging. A few years later, I can see that I wasn't being reasonable; that seventh in the nation and the all-American status it earned me, was nothing to apologize for. But I'd worked *so* hard for *so* long to create that opportunity for myself. To squander it (in my mind, that's what I'd done) felt like I'd thrown away all that work. The idea of going back to square one, doing that work all over again, just for the opportunity to *possibly* make it to the finals—which I might very possibly lose—filled me with a sense of hopelessness. I actually doubted if I could get through it, pay that price, and risk failing again.

The thought of it made me tired. I was emotionally and physically fatigued. I wanted no part of off-season workouts. I'd heard the expression "burnout." Now I had firsthand knowledge of exactly what it meant. It probably would've scared me, if I'd thought about it for very long. But I wasn't doing much deep thinking at that time. I was floating along in a kind of low-grade depression, numb to everything. Nothing affected me, emotionally. I was just . . . there.

I took a string of jobs at a series of wrestling camps. I needed the money—*we* needed the money—plus I liked working with kids, answering their questions, seeing the light go on for them as I taught them some of my favorite moves. It gave me a sense of being part of a community. The sport had given me a lot, and I liked the idea of giving back to that community, that wrestling family.

But the idea of going back to the Riches Wrestling

Complex—pumping iron, riding the bike, and climbing ropes with chains hanging off me and getting the crap beat out of me scrimmaging a bunch of guys twenty, thirty, and forty pounds heavier—had zero appeal. It's how I'd spent every summer for the last eight years, but this time around I couldn't stomach the thought of it. Like I said, I couldn't get far enough away from that room.

So I jumped at the chance to fly to Alaska with Coach Stith and Coach Charles to coach at a wrestling camp in Anchorage. Nathan Hoffer was a talented, incoming ASU freshman who'd won a couple state titles at East Anchorage High, where his dad, Mark, was head coach. During my time at the camp, the Hoffers were kind enough to put us up in their home. They offered me a bed in a nice RV out in front of their home, but mentioned, in the same breath, that I could expect nocturnal visits from elk and bear. I thanked them for the offer, then begged to sleep inside their home. I crashed on a couch.

When the camp was over, we drove three hours into the wilderness for a week of roughing it in the backcountry. I remember how incredibly beautiful it was—and surreal. Because it was summertime, and Alaska is so far north, the sun stayed up late into the night. (When we'd first arrived from the airport, Mrs. Hoffer had been mowing the lawn at 11:30 P.M.) I remember the majestic peaks and pine forests, the grassy tundra, the rivers swollen with snowmelt. It was a fantastic experience—for about a day and a half. After that, I wanted to go back to civilization.

I'm a city boy. I grew up in Southern California, then Arizona. I like being *warm*. (Even though it was June, the temperature dipped pretty drastically at night.) I feel like I suffer *enough* physical hardship, wrestling at a high level. And so, when I'm not doing that, I like being able to sit on the couch and watch television. I like taking meals at a table, with a roof over my head.

So, yeah, camping got old for me in a hurry. It helped that I wasn't the only one who felt that way. Coach Stith is also a bit of a city slicker, and sleeping on the ground lost its novelty for him, as it did for me, after one night. Coach Charles, on the other hand, loved every minute of it, and was forever exulting in and pointing out to us the glories of nature. I just wanted a shower. I wanted to watch *SportsCenter*.

Everybody else wanted to fish. That's why you go to Alaska in the summer, I found out. To cast your line in the river and hopefully reel in a big salmon or rainbow trout. We fished for a week. I caught one trout.

At least I didn't injure myself. One afternoon Brian *thought* he felt a fish strike his line, and jerked back hard on the rod—so hard that the hook came zipping back toward him, lodging itself in his eyelid. He didn't realize it at first. I had to be the one to tell him. As tough a guy as he was on the mat, he didn't take it that well. We had to calm him down a little. Eventually we got the hook out, without *too* much bloodshed, but Brian's enthusiasm for fishing took a pretty serious hit.

We saw a bunch of elk, and a cow moose with her calf. We never did see a bear, although one day when we were walking along the river, another group of campers told us we were in an area frequented by grizzlies. "You gotta be careful," one of the men said, "'cause they like to sneak up on ya."

We were pretty sure he was kidding, but I kept my head on a swivel the rest of the day. It made me think of the old joke about two campers in a tent that is attacked by a bear. One of the guys starts lacing up his running shoes, causing his companion to shout, "What are you doing? You can't outrun a bear!"

"I don't have to outrun the bear," he replies. "I just have to outrun you."

I didn't have any great epiphany in the wilderness. If anything, I was a little sadder coming out than I was going in. Cell phone reception is sketchy up there in the Yukon, but once in a while I'd get a couple bars and check in with my mom. During one of our conversations I was telling her about the whole novel experience, the camping out and fishing and sleeping in a tent. Normally she's bubbly and interested and full of questions. But on this day she was reserved, kind of quiet. I could tell something was going on at home.

When I got home, she confirmed my suspicion that Ron had left again. The previous time he'd bailed on us, Mom had told him, "If you do this again, we're done." And he'd cried, and sworn to her that he was changing. He was reading the Bible and praying. He was in a fellowship, and needed her help to get his relationship right with God. And she'd taken him back, warning, not for the first time, "If you do this again, we're done."

He did it again.

He gave her the news over the phone. It wasn't working out, he told her. He needed some space. This time, when my mom yelled at him to get out of her life, she meant it. This time, they actually *were* done.

A couple days after I got back, Ron called. He wanted to meet with me, so I invited him over to my apartment a few blocks from campus. We actually had a really good conversation. He told me that even though it wasn't working out with Judy, he still wanted to be in my life. It hurt, because they were splitting up. But it felt good to hear him tell me he still loved me, and that he wanted to stay in my life. Ron being gone would mean no more fighting, no more needing to call the cops when their arguments got too heated. My siblings and I wouldn't have to tiptoe around, worrying about triggering his temper.

Things wouldn't be ideal, but they would be better.

CHAPTER 13

Robles–Ashmore II

BY the end of July I was still on the fence, believe it or not, about coming back for my senior year. It was around this time that I got a call from Al Fuentes, who'd been fired along with Thom Ortiz after my sophomore season. Out of deference to the new coaching staff, Al had kept his distance for a year, but now was calling just to check in on me. I told him I was thinking about hanging up my shoes. He asked me to come by his office as soon as possible. I visited him the next day.

I was still mentally drained, I explained to him, still depressed, still convinced that I'd had my best shot at a national title and blown it. And Ashmore was in my head again. The coaches were going to make me earn my spot once more: I was going to have to beat him in a wrestle-off. I see now that they were just being fair. At the time it felt like they'd turned against me. I'd worked four-plus years to save, then build, the program, and they were making me feel expendable.

He listened to me, then sat quietly for a few moments. When he did speak, his words had a powerful effect on me:

"So you mean to tell me," he said, looking me dead in the eye, "that you've gone your entire life with one leg, not letting it slow you down, but you're going to let these guys break you?"

He leaned across his desk, fixing me with his gaze. "You have forgotten who you are. The hundred twenty-five-pound weight class—that's your spot. That's your room. This is your *season*. The fans that come into that arena—they come to see *you*." He was laying it on a little thick, but he made his point.

"You're letting outside, negative influences take away your power."

Just as he had helped me see my stepfather in a different, more compassionate light, he told me I needed to consider where Coach Charles was coming from. "He's got a lot going on. He's under a lot of pressure," Al explained to me. "He's doing what he thinks is the right thing, and you're taking it personally.

"Forget about him. Focus on yourself, and your

actions. This is your test—this is your moment to take your life back."

It was as if I'd been slapped in the face. For the first time in what felt like months, I was fully awake. And I went from being depressed to being angry. Ben is a good kid and a talented wrestler with the same goal I had. But when I pictured him challenging me for my spot, I thought, *How* dare *he? I'm here four years and now this kid's trying to come into my house and take over?* It made me furious with him, and that helped when it came time to take care of business.

I knew it was going to be close. Ben Ashmore never did give up more than a handful of points. And so of course the score was 0–0 going into the final period of our 2010 wrestle-off, dubbed Robles–Ashmore II by one of my friends. In previous seasons, going into the final round all tied up would've filled me with doubt and dread; it would've affected my performance. I had a tendency to wrestle defensively in those situations, to get away from my strengths—to give away my power. This time I felt calm, telling myself, *He can't beat me. This is my mat, my house. He can't take this from me.*

The rivalry between Ben and me had divided the room. You could hear it as we locked up on the mat: Some guys were pulling for me, some for him. *Let's go, Ashmore—you got this!* I know it wouldn't have broken

Coach Charles's heart to see me lose. He wanted me at 133. I was less of a threat to win a national title at that weight, but we'd score better in a lot of dual meets. I was even getting pressure from some of the other wrestlers on the team to relinquish my spot to Ben, to give it up without a fight.

Sorry, guys. Not happening. I could still hear Tom Brands, the Iowa coach, on the subject of entitlements: *He doesn't deserve anything. The only thing you deserve is what you earn.*

Let those guys give up their spots. Ben was going to have to take mine from me, which is precisely what he was trying to do in the final period of our second wrestle-off. He'd started on top, and as usual was coming after me with extreme aggression, pressing me forward, mashing me into the mat. Instead of dwelling on what a disaster it would be if I lost, I focused on slowing my breathing, which gave me the sense of slowing the match down. *Just wait for the opening*, I told myself. *It's gonna come.*

And then it came. With Ashmore digging into me from behind, I reached back, hooked his leg between the thigh and knee, and threw my hips hard and fast in the direction he was going, only faster. It was an exceptionally smooth, textbook Fat Man Roll, if I do say so myself, and Ben quickly found himself upside down, desperately trying to keep his shoulder blades off the mat. I couldn't pin him down long enough to earn near-fall points, but the ref did give me two for the reversal.

And that's how the match ended, 2–0. I was undefeated against Ashmore in wrestle-offs, but we weren't
finished with each other. Even as I blitzed my way through
the early season, destroying opponents, Coach Charles
talked about the possibility of another wrestle-off, midseason. I didn't let it get to me. I controlled the things I
could control. At some point, I started having fun again.

Against Oklahoma on November 18, I got a nice
hug from Coach Spates, who very nearly lured me to
his program two years earlier, then took apart his 125-
pounder, 16–1. In Fresno a few days later, at the NWCA
All-Star Classic presented by the U.S. Marine Corps, I
faced Zach Sanders of Minnesota, ranked third in the
country. I wasn't far behind, at number five.

My goal at this meet was to make a statement, to
serve notice to the other guys in the weight class that I
had no plans to fizzle out my senior season; that I would
be a force, nationally. I was also interested in a bit of
payback. I hadn't tangled with Sanders since the spring
of 2009. In the consolation semifinals at the NCAA tournament I'd thrashed him, 19–10. In the waning moments
of that match, after the ref had stopped the action, he
stomped my back while I was at his feet. He'd been as-
sessed a penalty point, and apologized to me later. I was
happy to accept that apology, which is not to say the
matter was forgotten.

The book on me was that I was easier to wrestle the
second time around, once you'd gotten the first match

under your belt, and the novelty of grappling with a one-legged dude had worn off. I'm sure that's true, but it cut both ways. The more I wrestled you, the more I figured you out. A few months before he stomped me in frustration, Sanders had dominated me 9–3 in Las Vegas. He'd come out guns blazing and pushed me all over the mat. Now in Fresno, two years later, I took him down in twenty-four seconds, then started turning him the way Pat Sajak spins the Wheel of Fortune. After three minutes I was up 14–0. We never made it into the third period; I teched him 20–2 in the second. It was the worst beating of his college career.

I wasn't that much stronger than I'd been as a junior, and hadn't picked up any new techniques. The truth is I hadn't trained with near the intensity of previous off seasons. The difference was mental. Before, I went into matches nervous, worried about losing, worried about my opponent's ranking and reputation. My attitude this season was more along the lines of *They need to worry about* me. I didn't care if you were ranked second or third or last in the country. I was going to tear you up, regardless.

This was how I thought: *You can't take me down, you can't stop me from taking you down. I can do whatever I want, to anybody. No matter what happens, I will come out of every position on top. I am too fast, and too strong. I am unstoppable.*

CHAPTER 14

I'll Do It

IT helped, during the first couple months of the season, that I was in a better place with my stepfather. Despite splitting up with my mother for good, he'd talked about wanting to stay in my life, strengthen our bond. When his relationship ended with a different woman, and he found himself without a roof over his head, I invited him to crash in my apartment, a few blocks off campus. It was around Christmas; I had a sad little fake tree in my "living room." It made me happy, coming home from practice, eating dinner with him. He'd made some mistakes—a lot of mistakes. My mother deserved better, frankly. But he was the only dad I'd ever known, and I loved him. I slept on the couch so he could have my bedroom.

He only stayed a couple weeks. We parted on good terms. It didn't last. Not because of anything he did or said to me. But he was cruel to my to mother, twisting things around to try to make their divorce seem like her fault. He began to wage a kind of low-grade psychological warfare on her, and I wouldn't stand for it. It was unacceptable, and I made the decision to cut him off.

By this time the wolf was truly at the door. The bank was in foreclosure proceedings on our house on East Harmony Road in Mesa. My mom had filed the paperwork for an extension, and then we caught a break: The bank screwed up its own paperwork, which bought us a few more months in the house. Judy was working part-time, but it was tough. She still had four kids at home. She was still selling her blood, still on food stamps, still gratefully accepting donations of food and money from the incredibly generous people at our church, the Calvary Chapel in Gilbert, Arizona, and from Pastor Jim Sheets of the New Life Christian Fellowship in West Covina, California. Pastor Jim is an old friend who's always been amazingly kind to us. We were blessed to have their help, because I was no longer kicking in.

Twice a week during my junior season, I would leave practice a half hour early to get to my job at the Rec Center, where I did homework between folding towels and handing out basketballs. Often, the part of practice

I missed was conditioning. Even though I'd come in early to do extra work, it concerned Coach Charles, who called me into his office to discuss the matter.

"Why do you need to work?" he'd asked me. "You're on a full scholarship, with a stipend for living expenses." I explained our family situation and told him that the money I earned went to my mother. It wasn't much—$125 every two weeks—but believe me, it helped. Coach Charles was totally understanding, and I'm grateful to him for that.

Going into my senior season, we met again. "You got one year left," he told me. "Whether or not you win a national title—and you have the talent to do it—there cannot be any doubts in your mind afterward that you gave it your best shot."

No part-time job, in other words. I agreed with him, as did Judy. Not only did I not get a job my senior season, I agreed to let Coach put me through a singular brand of torture that I ended up despising more than those old sandbag drills, more than the six-mile run that kicked off Hell Week.

In order for me to maneuver and glide around the mat from my preferred, low position—I liked to think of myself as an ice cube on a smooth surface—I basically used my arms as legs. On dual-meet days, when I only had to wrestle once, that wasn't an issue. At tournaments, where I'd sometimes have to wrestle three matches in a day, Shawn noticed that a certain level of fatigue set in. It happened late, in the semis or the finals of tournaments. My arms, chest, and shoulders—what I'd thought of as my strength—needed strengthening. Coach Charles had some very specific ideas on how I might do that.

I'd spent hours of my life—make that days, no, *weeks*—in the weight room, but never paid any attention to an unremarkable-looking piece of cardio equipment called the Arm Bike. I might have looked at it twice a year and thought, *Why?* I was about to find out.

While sitting on it as if on a bike, you grab the handles in front of you and pedal, using your arms. It sounds easy, and I'm sure it is, when you don't have Shawn Charles twisting the knobs, jacking up the resistance to inhuman levels while shouting, "All right, twenty seconds left in the period, you're riding him out, you can't let him go—CAN'T LET HIM GO! Gotta hold it at THIS LEVEL!"

This went on for several hours. Actually, it only *felt* like hours. We never went longer than seven minutes. Longest seven minutes of my life. The first time we did it, I fell backward onto the floor, arms outstretched, so spent I couldn't move my hands, willing myself not to puke, thinking I might pass out, looking at Coach with an expression that said, *I can't believe you just did that to me.*

He stood over me, looking down, and asked: "If I told you that's what it's going to take to win a national title, would you do it?"

My reply came out in a rasp: "I'll do it."

CHAPTER 15

Nationals

I blew into my senior season like a cyclone, flat-out overwhelming my early opponents. And yet I felt a twinge of nostalgia and sadness in early December at the Cliff Keen Invitational in Vegas. Dating back to high school, I'd wrestled in this town on at least seven occasions. This would probably be the last. Any feelings of sadness were crowded out on the mat: I won the title, beating my five opponents by a combined score of 71–5. I remember thinking, *Maybe there's something to this Arm Bike. . . .*

I improved on that at the Reno Tournament of Champions, where my combined score against five opponents was a combined 73–3. In our dual meet against dangerous Oklahoma State, the second-ranked team in the nation, I beat seventh-ranked Jon Morrison, 11–0. We lost our other nine matches. My 19–3 technical fall of Cal State Bakersfield's Tyler Iwamura was tougher than it looked. He was scrappy and fidgety—he moved around a lot. I shot his leg in the first period and took a kneecap in the forehead, and it stunned me. The rest of the match I was just a little off. After I won, the trainer took me to the back of the arena, where I started throwing up. I had mild concussion.

I finished the regular season with a record of 31–0, and led the nation in tech falls (wins by fifteen or more points), with twenty-two. I liked going for the tech instead of the pin. It was more fun (and less tiring) to rack up points on an opponent than it was to repeatedly engage him in a death struggle to stick his shoulder blades to the mat. Once I was a move or two away from that fifteen-point margin, I'd get the other guy in a headlock and try to pin him, or use some other move to finish him off. My winning streak was a topic that came up in my conversations with Al Fuentes, with whom I was once again speaking on a semi-regular basis. By taking my focus off the streak—so what? Who really cared about it? Of what real significance was it?—I didn't give it any power. After sweeping through the Pac-10 tournament, and earning the number one seed in the NCAA tournament, it felt like I was keeping most of my power for myself.

———

EARLY in the season, one of my teammates had handed me a wrestling magazine, open to a feature on Iowa's Matt McDonough. As a freshman the previous spring, he'd beaten Iowa State's Long in the finals to win the NCAA title. He talked in the story about his goal of defending his title. It was a pretty innocuous quote, but I underlined it, tore the article out of the magazine, and taped it to the wall in my locker. Every day before I went out to practice, I said hello to Mc-Donough, then went into the room with the ultimate goal of taking something from him.

He and Brandon Precin of Northwestern had gone at it three times that season. McDonough won twice. With those two bloodying each other, I slid past them in the rankings to the top spot. That didn't mean much—but it had its advantages. In the draw for the NCAA tournament, it put both those guys on the other side of the bracket. It meant I'd only have to scrap with one of them.

ESPN was all over the tournament broadcasting matches on ESPNU, ESPN3.com, and the main network. I was hearing from people back home that some of the announcers were skeptical of my high seeding. Yes, I was undefeated. But I hadn't wrestled the top guys in the country. In their eyes, I was still untested. I would have five matches to prove them wrong.

First Round

First up: Virginia's Matthew Snyder, a sophomore I'd beaten soundly in January. I now put that result out of my mind. A guy like Snyder is a dream crusher, unranked, not expected to do much at the tournament. So you know he's got nothing to lose, and is going to come out swinging. I expected nothing but a full-out fight from him, which is what I got. But I stuck to my process, did the things that had worked for me, and beat him 14–1.

It's customary, after finishing a match, to stick around and watch your upcoming opponent wrestle. It's just smart; it helps you prepare. I never did it, never stuck around. It drove my coaches crazy. As I explained to them, watching the other guy somehow helped him get inside my head before our match. I didn't want to watch him, didn't want to give him the chance to impress or intimidate me. So we worked out an arrangement. Coach Stith, my ex-teammate and one of Shawn's assistants, would scout the opponent, then shoot me a text with a few observations, reminders, and recommendations.

Second Round

Circles right with knee down, Stith cautioned me before my second round match with Harvard's Steven Keith. *Tries to lock on body as we finish . . . [Took a] shot off*

*the whistle (sneaky) . . . we need to be crisp finishing and
forceful on top.*

Keith had thrown a major scare into me, way back
in December, in Vegas. He took me down and scored
some back points on me. Instead of slowing my breathing, regrouping, I lost my temper and dug myself in
deeper. I beat him 7–4, but it was my narrowest victory
of the season. Looking at the brackets, people predicted
another close match.

Not if I could help it. I went after him with a fury,
got him down on the mat nine seconds in, then tilted
him four times to take a 14–0 lead. He didn't make it
out of the second period.

Quarterfinals

Tries to stay square, wrote Stith of my quarterfinal opponent, Oklahoma's Jarrod Patterson. *Right side wrist
control with headsnap-go-behind worked . . . ran out of
bounds constantly. Also grabbed both hands and kept way out
front (gave up lots of stalling calls)—handfight hard for
wrist control and for your positions. On feet be patient.*

I'd routed Jarrod twice this season. This time he
kept it closer—partly because I was rattled by something that happened moments before the match. Ever
since my sophomore year, I'd carried around a gallon
jug of water before each match. Freije had done it back
at Mesa High, and I did everything Freije did. After a

while it became an important part of my routine. I liked giving the jug a periodic squeeze; it reminded me of my grip strength. I thought of it as a briefcase. When I had it, I was all about business.

The jug was also a useful hat rack. That is, my protective headgear fit snugly over it, until it was time to snap on the gear and go to work. But now, when the ref called Patterson and me out onto the mat, I noticed for the first time that my headgear was missing its chinstrap. That had never happened before. While my coaches and I looked around the bench area, the ref warned us that I was in danger of forfeiting the match.

Luckily, I had a spare strap in my bag. But some residue from that short-lived panic followed me into the match. And Jarrod wrestled me smart, circling, keeping his distance, preventing me from shooting his legs. When I did finally take him down, I couldn't turn him. Midway through the match I only led 5–3. But Coach Charles had prepared me for this sort of war of attrition. There were going to be guys who refused to allow me to hit the ball and chain; who would not allow me to turn them into a piñata, spilling points all over the mat. I would have to outlast them, find another way to win. In the third I notched another takedown, earned another point for riding time, and won 9–3. This was where I'd flamed out a year earlier. Finally, I'd broken through.

Semis

He will try front-headlock-run-around while grabbing your foot, predicted Stith of Utah Valley's Ben Kjar (pronounced "car"). *Stay away from underhooks and headlocks.*

I'd wrestled Ben a lot over the years, and we'd become friends. He was short, compact, extremely smart, and scary strong. Normally I like to handfight with guys. I'll bait them into taking one of my wrists. Once they grab it, I'll take it back, then snag *theirs*. That didn't work with Ben. When he got one of my wrists, it was really hard to get it back.

He was one of those guys I just didn't match up well against. He stayed super-low, and was good at taking control of my head. A year earlier he'd caught me with a throw that put me on my back. If time hadn't expired in the period, he would've pinned me.

And he was on the roll of his life in St. Louis. He'd already beaten the fourth and fifth seeds, and his confidence was sky-high. As I had in nearly every match that season, I made a conscious effort to slow my breathing. *There is no hurry*, I told myself. *You'll get your chance.* The first period ended scoreless, but I'd racked up two minutes of riding time.

No score in the second. It was a pitchers' duel.

This was the sort of competition I'd often found a way to lose earlier in my career: a close match going into the final two minutes. But I opened the period with an escape—now it was 1–0—then hit him with a sweep single: Circling right, I shot in on his leg. He tried to counter. With one hand on his wrist and another around his waist I executed a hip throw, and that's where I got my points. It was the only takedown of the match, which I won, 4–2. Unless you were a coach or some kind of wrestling purist, that match was like watching paint dry. To Coach Charles and me, it was a masterpiece. From the first week I'd worked with him, Shawn had driven this message home: If I wanted to be a national champion, I was going to have to learn how to finish close matches. I would have to learn to ride guys out, to stay on top of them even when I couldn't turn them. We worked hard on that, and it was paying off. I couldn't help thinking, after that match, that I'd won it on the Arm Bike.

Dating back to my freshman year, when I got a standing ovation after losing in overtime to Gardner of Stanford, I'd had a strong connection with the fans at the NCAAs. They kind of adopted me. It was fun for me. I fed off it, and I think it helped my wrestling. We had great fans at Arizona State; we just never had that many of them.

After each match, my walk back to the tunnel took me past the fans seated in the front row. They would congratulate me and tell me good job; I would smile back and thank them. After my first win, I held up four fingers, explaining, "Gotta win four more." After my second victory, I held three fingers. People caught on. As I went crutching past after beating my buddy Kjar, I saw a long row of people looking at me, smiling, holding up a single finger.

HE *is deceptively strong. You have to be stronger. He likes fireman's [hold]. Stay away from giving him high elbow control in neutral position. Wrestle hard in your best positions. Win.*

This was Stith on Iowa's Matt McDonough, the defending national champion, who'd edged Precin in the other semifinal. I had indoctrinated myself in the lore and history of Hawkeyes wrestling and had walked around in high school with a Hawkeyes ballcap. In those days, if I could've chosen one school to attend, one program to join, it would've been Iowa. Now this son of Marion, Iowa, stood between me and my dream.

Freije had been the one who turned me on to Iowa wrestling, who reveled in the program's signature aggression and intensity. I remember going over to his house to watch the national finals on TV. Both of us had dreamed of walking out of that tunnel in the Parade of Champions, then wrestling for a national title. After nine years of work, the moment was upon me. It was scary and exciting at the same time.

All the finalists weighed in the next morning at the arena. Then we had the day to ourselves. We weren't wrestling until that evening. The coaches prefer that we spend that time resting in our hotel rooms. But that would've driven me nuts. Plus, my mom and my siblings had flown out (as had Freije and coaches Williams and DiDomenico from Mesa High). I wanted to push the tournament out of mind for an hour or two. So we drove over to the Philadelphia Museum of Art, where Nicholas ran the steps, just like Rocky. (I was saving my strength.) We had a nice lunch, but by the time our food was served, I was a mess—nervous, preoccupied, trying not to get crushed by the magnitude of the moment.

We weren't in the best part of Philly, so I walked with my mother a couple blocks to where the rental car was parked. I was so nervous by this time that I was fighting back tears. I was afraid she would ask me how I was doing, and I'd lose it. Mom knew that, of course, so she didn't ask.

CHAPTER 16

Finals

THE warm-up area was beneath the concourse, away from the eyes of the spectators. It was a large space with a bunch of wrestling mats lying side by side. There was plenty of room for everyone. So it seemed strange to me that McDonough and some of his boys kept walking past the spot where I was warming up, staring at me. I knew all about the Iowa philosophy: They don't just want to beat you—they want to humiliate you, to make you regret ever having taken up the sport. As I noted, a Hawkeye heavyweight had said in *The Season*: "I think wrestling's a good sport because you can break somebody. You can break their spirit; you can make them be a different person for the rest of their life."

Still, I was surprised that McDonough would attempt this gamesmanship with me. I mean, I was a fifth-year senior! Did he really think his little mind games would work on me?

Okay, they worked a little. He got me thinking. *Maybe the skeptics are right. Maybe the guys I've beaten this year* aren't *that great. This guy's a national champion. He's already beaten Escobedo, who I could never solve; he's never lost a match in four tries against Andrew Long, who knocked me out of this tournament last year. He's the best wrestler at the best program in NCAA history.*

Doubts started creeping in. *Am I overmatched?*

Keeping a close eye on me was Coach Charles, who came over to take my emotional temperature. Shawn was a four-time all-American who'd twice made it to the finals. He later told me that he'd been watching McDonough play mind games, watching the pressure build up in me. He asked himself, *If I was in that position again, what would I want to hear?*

He asked me a question: "What do you think you need to do to go out there and have success; to win this thing?"

I wasn't really thinking straight at that moment, so I gave him some boilerplate response that I thought he wanted to hear about working hard and being tough. "No. What you have to do," he said as he stepped in closer and slowed his speech, "is: Do. What. You. Do.

When your positions are there, you *take* them, just like in any other match."

That stayed with me. Later, in the tunnel, just before the announcer called my name, I was so nervous it felt like my head was going to explode. Shawn was right there. I asked him a kind of inane question: "Should I put my headgear on?"

"No," he told me. "Do what you normally do."

And so I crutched out into the arena, sans headgear, as usual. There were twenty thousand people in that building, and the ovation was thunderous; I felt it as much as I heard it. And I went through my usual routine. I hung out by the edge of the mat, in my coaches' corner. I took my shirt off, tugged my kneepad into position, and took a final swig from the jug, just so I didn't get cotton-mouthed out there. I strapped on my headgear, then stalled just a little, waiting until McDonough ventured out to the center of the mat. *Let him wait for me.* After lingering with the coaches for a few more moments, I joined the defending champion.

HE came at me like a buzz saw at the whistle, just as I knew he would, smacking my headgear, backing me off, pushing me out of the little circle before we settled into a stalemate, each of us trying to control the other's hands, our flat backs forming a kind of table. I made a conscious effort to slow my breathing. *Just like any other match*, I told myself. *Relax. When you see an opening, pull the trigger.*

A half-minute into the match, I saw an opening. With my right hand pinning his left wrist to the mat, I swung around his body, got behind him, and, after a ten-second struggle, completed the takedown. I relaxed at that moment; it was when I realized that I wasn't wrestling a tradition or a logo; I wasn't wrestling Terry or Tom Brands, who sat dourly a few feet away as I took that 2–0 lead. I was wrestling a true sophomore who seemed confused and off-balance, who wasn't out of my league, after all.

With McDonough on his stomach and me on McDonough, my universe became very small. My sole purpose, at that point, was to capture his left wrist. He writhed and twisted and crossed his arms, to repel me, to deny me the wrist, but with a couple minutes left in the period, I clamped on. "This is where McDonough doesn't want to be," said ESPN analyst Jeff Blatnick. "You want to keep your wrists away, and right now Robles has the cross-wrist."

My next mission was to drag and pull and roll that wrist from above his shoulders down toward his stomach. The Brandses were quite vocal about the importance of him not giving up the wrist, and—once he gave it up—not allowing me to pull it down. It was slow, painstaking work, like a boa ingesting a bunny rabbit. Every inch he gave me was an inch he never got back. I worked methodically. I still had half the period. I was in excellent spirits. When I'm able to get the cross-wrist, then pull it down to around the opponent's pectoral, it feels like Christmas morning. I don't mean to sound overconfident, but the points are as good as on the board. It's only a question of how many.

With one hand on his wrist and the other on his forearm, I pushed off with my foot, arching my leg toward the ceiling like the hand of a clock, flipping myself and McDonough, who found himself looking up at the lights, flailing to keep his shoulder blades off the mat. The ref rung up two near-fall points. Now I was up 4–nada, and the crowd was going nuts. I remember being in a similar situation in Iowa City, battling Charlie Falck as nearly fifteen thousand fans shouted for him, and against me. We were a long way from Carver-Hawkeye Arena.

He flipped back onto his stomach, but I stayed on top. The refs won't give you points for a new tilt unless you release the hold and start a new one, so I try to make it really obvious when I'm releasing a hold. Passing his wrist from my right hand to my left, I waved briefly at the ref with my right. Passing it back to my right, I then signaled with my left. *New hold*.

We were under a minute left in the period. Four points didn't feel like enough against McDonough. Yeah, I had his wrist now, but I had a feeling he wasn't going to give it up again. I needed more points. Time for the ball and chain.

Now he was on his side, left arm extended over his head. McDonough began pinwheeling around the mat, desperate to escape. Taking control of his left wrist again, I collapsed it down toward his abdomen, then transferred possession of that wrist to my other hand. Sending my left arm up between his splayed legs—*Beg your pardon!*—I returned the captured wrist to my left, pulling it between his legs like a tail. The fuse was lit; it was now simply a matter of when the bomb would go off.

The bend in his elbow made an inviting target—a handle—for my right arm. But as I tried to thread the keyhole, McDonough pushed urgently away from me. *Have it your way*, I thought, swinging my leg once again to the rafters, using his momentum to flip him once again onto his back, reigniting the crowd and racking up three more near-fall points.

The period ended 7–0. Time to overhaul my strategy. Instead of going on the attack, I needed to be smart and defensive. McDonough had trailed Northwestern's Brandon Precin by three points in the final period of their match two months earlier, but trapped the Wildcat in a headlock, then put him on his back and pinned him.

MCDONOUGH and I were butting heads a minute or so into the second when he whipped around to his left, grabbing for some purchase—a limb, some nylon, a kneepad—but whiffed. "A fine example right there, Jeff," said ESPN's Todd Harris. "As McDonough was trying to arch around . . . there was nothing to grab!"

Earlier, one of the talking heads had explained to the audience that in going up against me, McDonough would be forced to "throw out everything he knows . . . because it's different, wrestling Anthony Robles . . . you have to create a new game plan."

"His strength is off the charts," added another. "So you gotta think, *How good would he be if he had both legs? Or maybe he wouldn't be as good as he is now.*"

I don't "gotta think" about how good a wrestler I might be if I'd come out of the womb with four limbs. Because I didn't. I'm dealing with the hand I was dealt, just as the guys who have to wrestle me must deal with the hand they're dealt.

"I don't think I would ever say that it's an advantage for someone to have only one leg," says Stanford's Tanner Gardner, who always wrestled me tough and smart. "But facing him forces you to adapt to his strategy. In that sense he does have an advantage, but that's not to minimize the hard work that Anthony's done, because he's obviously a great technician, and is extremely strong.

"It took a lot of time to prepare for him," added Gardner, who had teammates tape their legs together, to better simulate what it would be like to face me. "Preparing for normal guys we might spend fifteen minutes, covering their offense, their tendencies, what they do. But when you wrestle a guy like Anthony you spend hours preparing to neutralize his strengths. Because the things he does well, he does *really* well. When you're competing against someone else, you can win with conditioning and brute strength. You beat Anthony with strategy."

Or not. After a scoreless second period, I was two minutes from a national title. I knew McDonough would be looking for a big move, a Hail Mary. He started on top, and quickly circled to the front of my head. As he worked toward my right side—the side with no leg—I guessed that he was trying to set me up for a Gator Roll, in which you trap the head and arms of an opponent then whip him around onto his back. Hooking my right arm behind his right leg, I kept him from "turning the corner" and getting behind me.

With just under seventeen seconds to wrestle, I was (quite deservedly) penalized a point for stalling. I could live with that. I couldn't live with getting head-locked and pinned in the waning seconds of the match. As the clock bled out, McDonough started choking me— inadvertently, I'm sure—in a desperate effort to pry me off the mat. Beneath him, I was already smiling, thinking, *Dude can choke me all he wants, because I'm about to become a national champion!*

I stayed on my knee for a moment, head on the mat, letting it soak in. Then I raised my arms and pointed to the heavens, offering thanks to God for giving me this opportunity. Meanwhile the ESPN cameras cut to my mother, going berserk way up in Section 223. She could not have been farther away, and still have been in the same building with me. But we were never closer than in that moment. She'd raised me with my head in the clouds, raised me to believe I could do anything I wanted. This wasn't my victory. It was ours.

I shared a quick handshake and nod with Mc-Donough, who I respect immensely. He sprinted off the mat and was almost to the tunnel before the referee raised my arm. That's the Iowa way.

THE Arizona State way is to show a bit more emotion. I leapt into the arms of Coach Charles, who challenged me and angered me, but who also rounded and completed me as a wrestler, gave me the tools to become a champion. He was happy for me, but more than that, he later told me, he was relieved. He knew how much pressure I'd put on myself, how empty and disappointed I'd have felt to have come so far and fallen short.

His workday was only half done. Later that evening, my teammate Bubba Jenkins wrestled for the 157-pound crown against David Taylor, an undefeated freshman from Penn State (and the winner, incidentally, of that season's Dan Hodge Award—wrestling's Heisman Trophy). The Nittany Lions fans booed Bubba, who'd transferred to ASU from Penn State. They piped down halfway through the second, when he caught Taylor in an inside cradle, bending the freshman into a human horseshoe for twenty or so seconds before spinning sideways in a sudden, spectacular, *inspired* roll that resulted in a pin for my teammate. Whereas I jumped into Shawn's arms, Bubba took a flying leap and nearly sailed over our coach, who only stands 5'7". Bubba somehow ended up on top of Shawn, who then spun him like a propeller blade, before my boy Brian Stith got in on the act, at which point they both held him up. It was crazy. It was beautiful. The program that had been declared dead for a week and a half three years earlier had produced two national champions.

It was a great night to be an Arizona State Sun Devil.

I guess I should've gone to my trusty gallon jug more often, because when the time came for me to produce a sample for the NCAA's drug testers, my cup did not exactly runneth over. But the officials were cool about it; while I waited to get more hydrated, I found my family in the upper reaches of the arena and shared a lot of hugs. Chris Freije was there, too—by this time he'd taken a gig as an assistant wrestling coach at Mesa State in Colorado—as were coaches Williams and DiDomenico from my high school. It made me happy, knowing they knew that *I* knew that none of this could've happened without their inspiration and help.

I stuck around for the awards presentation and ended

up with two trophies, one for my title and another for being chosen as the tournament's most outstanding wrestler. After one more interview with ESPN, my family and friends and I headed over to this really cool restaurant on Chestnut Street, a converted bank called the Union Trust Steakhouse. (To get to the restrooms, you head downstairs, through the former vault. *That* was badass.) When we rolled up, some people outside the restaurant congratulated me; they told me they'd seen me on ESPN. We were late, because of the awards ceremony, but they kept the kitchen open for us. Everyone was incredibly nice, and I've never had a better steak, although I didn't finish mine. I was so happy and *relieved* and filled with joy that it felt as if I spent most of that meal floating, over the table, among the chandeliers, looking down on the trophies someone had turned into centerpieces, looking down at the people I loved.

COOL thing about wrestling: Once the season's over, we drop the macho posturing. A certain level of hostility is ingrained in the sport. We're taught from the moment we first put on the headgear that our opponent is out to take what we want, to crush our dreams and humiliate us in front of our families. He's not a guy just like you, trying to keep his girlfriend happy while juggling schoolwork and family and the demands of an incredibly difficult sport. He's The Enemy. To justify the sacrifice and suffering they demand, a lot of coaches go a little overboard describing what's at stake. *Win you live. Lose you die.*

But who can sustain that intensity all year round? Not even Tom Brands, it turned out. After the medal ceremony, I was doing a quick interview with a wrestling website when I felt a tap on my shoulder. It was Coach Brands. He looked me in the eye and told me, "Good job."

"Wow," said the guy conducting the interview, "that was pretty cool, right?"

That was extremely cool.

The party was in full swing when I got back to the hotel, the lobby jammed with short guys with distressed ears and unnaturally low body fat, mingling, laughing, making up for lost time. I walked through the doors and was instantly embraced, congratulated, regaled, slapped on the back. I was with my people, my tribe. I was two thousand miles from Arizona, but I was home. I didn't get up to my room till 4 A.M.

I rose with a start, and immediately checked to see if the trophies were still on the dresser where I'd left them. I had this fear that it was still only the second day of the tournament, that I still had to win four more matches. But there they were, exactly where I'd left them. It was real. I'd won the national title. It wasn't a dream.

And then I remembered. Before collapsing a few hours earlier, I'd gone on Facebook and been stunned to see that I had five thousand friend requests. A bunch of people told me my name had been a trending topic on Twitter. Even before sleep found me that morning, I knew I was entering a new, exciting phase. I knew that my life would never be the same.

CHAPTER 17

Unstoppable

I was so hungover the next morning that I nearly threw up on the way to the airport. It wasn't due to alcohol—I'm not a drinker—but because I'd eaten like a man just out of prison: cookie-dough ice cream and pizza, washed down with way too much root beer. My body wasn't used to all that grease and sugar and fat.

When I turned on my phone in the hotel that morning, it blew up with texts and voice mails. I had more interview requests than I could respond to. ESPN wanted me to come up to its Bristol, Connecticut, headquarters, CBS and *Sports Illustrated* wanted to do features on me. But at that point I just wanted to go home and sleep in my own bed. I hadn't seen my dogs in a week.

That first week back home I just stopped carrying the phone around with me. I put it on silent mode and left it on the table in my apartment. It was out of control. I couldn't deal. I've been answering e-mails constantly since that time, but they come in faster than I can reply, so I'm still about a thousand behind. The sports information office at Arizona State was inundated with interview requests, as was my mom, who by this time was working at ASU in its office of undergraduate admissions. The first morning she got back to the office, her supervisor told her Disney had called. There were invitations to speak, messages from talk show booking agents. There were offers of free travel. Several entrepreneurs wanted me to make DVDs. Someone pitched a clothing line. Others wanted to use my name to pitch their products.

In those early days, my mom was more than happy to be the bad guy, to say "Thanks, but no thanks," and hang up.

As time passed, I knew I wanted to be a motivational speaker, and it was good fortune to be introduced to Joel Weldon, a highly regarded speaker and speaking coach, who is based in Phoenix. Joel helped me land some gigs at local high schools and junior highs. Now that I was finished wrestling, it was okay for me to accept a speaking fee. I was getting $150 here, $250 there—sometimes as much as $500 for a speech! Between my speaking engagements and an internship in the marketing department of an "assessment software" company, I was rollin'!

And that was a good thing, because my mom and siblings had been served an official "move-out" date by the bank. After giving Judy a couple of extensions, the bank had refused to modify the loan, and then they foreclosed. More hard times came a couple of weeks after that when Judy totaled her Jeep on the freeway on her way to work.

She called one day in May, crying on the phone. "Do you have time to talk?" she asked through her tears. My first thought was, *Here we go again: Some fresh bad news about Ron.*

I was wrong—she was crying happy tears. Mom was on the line with a producer from ESPN. I jumped on a three-way call. The network wanted to honor me with the Jimmy V Award for Perseverance, to be presented in July during the ESPYs, the Oscars of the sporting universe. Jim Valvano was the former NC State hoops coach whose acceptance of the Arthur Ashe Courage Award at the 1993 ESPYs—eight weeks before he died of cancer—set the bar for inspirational speeches.

The producer asked us to keep that news on the down low. We made plans for a film crew to come visit, for a five-minute piece that would air during the ESPYs. By this time, I'd hired a manager, which was easier said than done. We talked to IMG, CAA, Octagon, William Morris, and probably thirty other agents and lawyers and producers who wanted to work with us.

But meanwhile, we heard about a guy named Gary

Lewis, who worked with Michael Jordan, Drew Brees, Charles Barkley. Gary had a reputation for integrity, but when my mom got him on the phone, he told her he wasn't taking new clients. Judy liked that. She got him to agree to at least talk to me. And what do you know, after my phone conversation with Gary, I had a manager!

Gary knew how big the Jimmy V Award was. He also knew that I'd be asked to deliver an acceptance speech. That speech would serve as an opportunity to give thanks and also to deliver my message of hope and perseverance to an international television audience. That moment could serve as a springboard into the next phase of my life, so we wanted to get it right.

ESPN was gracious enough to allow me to bring my whole family with me to the ESPYs, so we all flew to L.A. and were met at the airport by our own driver. He met us in one of those oversize Mercedes vans, which to me was even cooler than a limo. At the W Hotel on Hollywood Boulevard, the hotel staff all knew my name— "Pleasure to have you here, Mr. Robles. . . . Good afternoon, Mr. Robles"—which was weird but also cool. ESPN got us *three* rooms at the W so that all the kids had a bed, which is definitely not how we're accustomed to traveling.

Next, we were guided through a series of "studios" full of free merchandise and gift cards. As soon as I walked in, I would be "announced." I'm not kidding, it was someone's job to actually say, in an official voice, "three-time all-American and NCAA wrestling champion Anthony Robles!" I never did quite get used to that.

Then a person would provide a description of the gift cards and merchandise they were about to give me. It felt like I was on a game show. They'd pile me up with all kinds of free stuff from wireless headphones, sunglasses, luggage, and video games, to gift certificates to spas, hotels, and resorts. I felt like a Miami Hurricane football player. It was a good thing I had my brothers and sister with me because I would've had trouble carrying all the stuff. When we got back up to our rooms, we laid out all the gifts on one of the beds. I had a great time divvying them up among all of my siblings. It felt like Christmas in July.

The real fun was the people-watching. I was amazed and humbled by how many of them knew my story. Adrian Peterson of the Minnesota Vikings introduced himself, as did Blake Griffin and some of the Dallas Mavericks. I'm a fan of Mixed Martial Arts fighting, so I was thrilled that Georges St-Pierre knew who I was. GSP overcame a difficult childhood to become the welterweight champion of the UFC. I met Urijah "the California Kid" Faber, an ex–UC Davis wrestler who transitioned to Mixed Martial Arts and, three years later, had climbed to the top of the rankings.

I shook hands and accepted congratulations from a lot of people I knew were *somebody*—I just wasn't sure who. Falling into that category was a cheerful, buffed-out guy who made small talk with us then moved along. One of my little brothers rushed over and asked, "Do you know who that was? That was Kirk Morrison!" An NFL linebacker, Morrison was one of the Raiders' leading tacklers in the years before 2010, when he was traded to Jacksonville.

The next thing I knew, my mom was shouting down the hallway, "Hey, Morrison!" Smiling, he came back. We apologized for not recognizing him right away and let him know how serious we were about following the Silver and Black. True, Kirk was no longer a Raider. But it didn't seem like the right time or place for us to discuss our strict policy toward ex-Raiders: Once you leave the team, your jersey goes to the farthest recess of our closet or, more often, is donated to the homeless.

We all got pictures with Kirk, who was fun and gracious and kind. And then we let him go on his way. I still think that was the highlight of the weekend for my mom. Of course, she met Tim Tebow and found him perfectly pleasant. Though for all his charms, unfortunately, it was impossible for Judy to harbor genuine affection for him. Raiders don't mix well with Denver Broncos.

It was difficult for me to truly let go and enjoy myself and the moment, because I had a speech to give. While it seemed like a big jump—from addressing students in the gym at Chandler High in Arizona to giving a speech to some of the most famous athletes in the world before millions of TV viewers—it really helped that I had *some* experience at public speaking. That, at least, is what I kept telling myself in the days before the show.

Gary had hooked me up with Dan Clark, a giant in the public-speaking world. Dan had helped me with my acceptance speech, and I'd rehearsed it over and over. I was as prepared as I'd ever been for any wrestling match. But there was something about meeting my fellow nominees (they weren't athletes, they were celebrities!) and then seeing the stage at the Nokia Theatre (like the deck of an aircraft carrier!) that made me really nervous. A couple of hours before the event, I was told that Jay Leno would be presenting me with the award. That's when the butterflies in my stomach turned into seagulls.

Finally, the town cars and limos all pulled up to the Nokia Theatre, everyone had their moment on the red carpet, and the show began. Before I knew it, the time had come for the Jimmy V Award. There was Leno, striding across the stage—he looks even bigger in person. "Some people spend their entire lives wishing for amazing things they'll never get," he began. "Others just focus on doing amazing things with whatever they have."

I liked that. After describing my wrestling accomplishments, Leno mentioned, almost casually, "Anthony was born with only one leg, and that should matter to you, even if it never really mattered to him."

That was the producer's signal to cue up the short

feature ESPN had put together. They did a beautiful job. The piece was about me, but my mom was the star: "I remember the first time I saw Anthony wrestle. I went into the stands and my son threw down his crutches and he hopped to the middle of the mat. And there's this scrawny little kid—that's my son!—and I was so proud of him. But this woman was laughing, and it broke my heart."

What Mom neglected to mention was that she got up in that lady's face like Kirk Morrison filling the A-gap on the goal line. But she was on a roll. And the camera *loved* her. (Can I say that about my mom?)

She continued: "When he first started it was like, 'Oh, poor thing. Good for him, he's trying. He's got one leg. He's at a disadvantage.' And then as he started winning, it was, 'Oh, he's got an advantage because he's got all that upper body strength, and people can't get low enough.'

"No. The kid just figured out how to beat you guys."

Then they rolled tape of the highlights from my match with McDonough, which I might have enjoyed more if it didn't feel like 110 degrees backstage and I wasn't one minute from walking out and having to give the biggest speech of my life. One lady was fanning me with a clipboard, while someone from makeup put powder on my forehead so I wouldn't be too shiny. And then it was time for me to take that long walk across the stage to where Jay was waiting. And as I walked out under those bright lights, I prayed: *God, don't let me screw this up.*

But something happened that helped put me at ease, that allowed me to relax just a little. As I approached Jay, everyone in the theater rose and applauded. And applauded. And applauded some more. I mean, they wouldn't sit down! Serena Williams and Lindsey Vonn and a bunch of Packers and Mavericks and Julius Erving—Dr. J himself! It was wild to see them and re- alize, *Wow, they're cheering for me!*

But that delay also helped me remember what I'd rehearsed. Yes, there were teleprompters available, but I preferred to almost memorize my speech and make eye contact with the audience rather than the prompter. It just feels more authentic.

Once the time came, the words tumbled out of me, no problem. My first order of business was to give props to my mom—I'd always wanted to do that on national TV:

"When I was born, my birth dad immediately bailed. I was born with one leg, and my mom could've walked away, just given me up for adoption. But she didn't. She taught me to never let what I cannot do interfere with what I can do. And she didn't protect me from pain and failure, because she knew it would make me stronger.

"Even when my mom got sick at the beginning of my sophomore year in college, and my stepdad walked out on the family, and we lost our home, and I wanted to quit wrestling to get a job to help pay the bills, my mom refused to let any of us give up. And here I am today: national champion."

I didn't go easy on Ron, did I? He hasn't spoken to me since. He put the word out that he wasn't happy with me for making that reference to him. Oh well. I'm not happy with him for a lot of decisions he made when I was growing up. I put a lot of thought about whether or not I'd mention him in the speech. But my story is all about overcoming obstacles, and there were times—not always, but a lot of times—that my stepfather created obstacles for me and our family.

Dan Clark is always telling me that anger is corrosive; that bearing a grudge is like drinking poison and expecting the other person to die. I'm not angry at Ron anymore. Just disappointed.

I thanked three people in that speech. One of them was Judy. The other two were Bobby Williams and Chris Freije, "who took me under their wrestling wings," I said, "to push me every step of the way." It should be noted, in Freije's case, that he also bodily *threw* me part of the way.

And then it was time to read the poem Dan had written for me, which I love, because it captures who I am. I shared it earlier and am sharing again now:

Every soul who comes to earth

With a leg—or two—at birth

Must wrestle his opponents knowing

It's not what is, it's what *can be* that measures worth.

Make it hard, just make it possible

And through pain I'll not complain,

My spirit is unconquerable.

Fearless I will face each foe, for I know

I am capable. I don't care what's probable.

Through blood, sweat, and tears

I am Unstoppable.

As it turned out, I was just getting started.

FOR a guy who wrestled nine years, my ears aren't bad. The right one flares out about 25 degrees, and catches the breeze more than my left, which lies flat against my head like a normal ear, although it is a tiny bit mashed-looking. As a result of repeated blows, a lot of guys in this sport end up with permanently scarred and swollen (aka "cauliflower") ears. They see their damaged ears as a badge of honor, and I get that. Like them, I'm proud to be a member of a special fraternity. But I was always meticulous about practicing with my headgear. I didn't want to go through life with people staring at my ears, although, come to think of it, it might have given them something to stare at other than my missing leg.

My hands, more than my ears, tell the story of my

wrestling. From my fingers down to my lower forearms, I've got this tracery of scars—souvenirs of nicks and scrapes inflicted by opponents desperately trying to free their wrists. With their free hand they would pinch and gouge me, bend my fingers backward. Compared to the torments we put ourselves through in the wrestling room, that pain barely rated as a nuisance. I welcomed it.

In my new line of work, my hands are used to tell a story as well. I use them to get a point across, to gesticulate. Even before I stopped wrestling, I'd felt the desire to share my message of hope, to inspire people to overcome the obstacles in their lives—to feel unstoppable. I wanted to be a motivational speaker.

The morning after the ESPYs I flew to Michigan to give a speech in Kalamazoo. If the NCAAs had markedly heightened my profile, the ESPYs put me into orbit. I was deluged with messages—texts, e-mails, voice mails—all over again. Exciting things started happening. I signed with Nike. That company had never signed someone whose competitive career was already over, but the Nike folks made an exception for me. Gary fielded more calls and offers from movie studio executives and producers.

While in New York City on a business trip, I was invited to meet the Jets before a preseason game. I was intrigued by their head coach, Rex Ryan, a big man with a bigger personality. I'd been told that Coach Ryan uses some pretty salty language, but he kept it PG around me.

I got to chat with Mark Sanchez, the Jets quarterback. Great guy. Judy had taken a look at the 2011 schedule and knew the Jets were visiting Oakland in September. A friend of hers, a Jets fan, had predicted that Sanchez would carve up Oakland's secondary. Like the Raiders fan she is, my mother promised, "We're gonna mess that pretty boy up." I didn't share that with Mark.

The Jet I really bonded with was LaDainian Tomlinson. I loved how genuine and down to earth he was. LT knew that I was a Christian. During warm-ups he asked me to deliver the team's "shower prayer."

Not long before kickoff, a lot of the players gather, of all places, in the shower to say their pregame prayer. One by one, the space filled up with giant men who looked even bigger because, by now, they were in full gear. I've never felt so small! When the time was right, we all joined hands and bowed our heads. I kept it short and sweet. Even when I was wrestling, I never prayed for victory. It wouldn't have felt right. Standing there among the showerheads, I asked the Lord to protect my brothers; I prayed for the angels to cover them with their wings while they competed, to keep them safe. I felt really blessed to have had that opportunity.

AS more and more speaking offers flooded in, we raised my rate. Early that fall, I was recruited to join the prestigious Washington Speakers Bureau, whose clients include Ted Koppel, Condoleezza Rice, George W. Bush, Tom Brokaw . . . and now, yours truly.

My first gig for the WSB was in Hershey, Pennsylvania. I'd be giving a speech to the corporate management team for Wells Fargo Bank. I was tense, and not just because bankers aren't known for being the liveliest, most outgoing people in the world. They're bankers! They're supposed to be cautious and conservative. But the same qualities that make them good stewards of our money can also make them a tough audience.

This being my first-ever speech for the new agency, the Washington Speakers Bureau was especially interested in how I did. Present in the hall that night was Steve Sobel, a senior vice president at the WSB. He was there to hold the hands of the Wells Fargo bigwigs— the bank is an important client. But he was also there to evaluate my performance.

Back in California, Gary, my manager, was nervous, too. He knew when I was scheduled to start speaking in Hershey, and he knew roughly when I'd be finished. It was at precisely that moment that his phone rang. It was Sobel, who was shouting to make himself heard over the crowd noise. For fourteen years, the Bureau had been sending speakers to this event—talents like Colin Powell, Tony Blair, and a lot of other serious luminaries. In all that time, the bankers had never given anyone a standing ovation.

Sobel called during the third standing ovation. All

over the room, he reported, there were grown men weeping. "This is unbelievable," he exclaimed. I was off to a good start with the Washington Speakers Bureau.

But my favorite gig of the year took place in Northern California in late November. This one I didn't need the WSB to arrange. Back in March at the NCAA tournament in Philadelphia, I was warming up for my finals match when someone passed me a phone out of the stands. During one of my earlier matches, the camera had zoomed in on the Raiders tattoo on my left shoulder. People started banging the drums in Raider Nation, e-mailing one another. Next thing I knew I was handed a phone by the cousin of an Oakland assistant coach. Then came one of the more surreal moments in a surreal year.

"Anthony, this is Hue Jackson, head coach of the Raiders," said the voice at the other end of the line. "We wanted to let you know that we're watching your matches, we're pulling for you, and we want to bring you out here with your family next season." The Raiders had actually followed all the proper channels, contacting my coach and my mom first. (Think she was a little jacked up to get that call?)

I thanked Coach Jackson, hung up, smiled, shook my head, and tried to put the conversation out of my mind. I still had to wrestle Matt McDonough.

True to their word, the Raiders flew us all out for Oakland's late-November game against the Chicago

Bears. We were met at the airport, then driven to the team headquarters in Alameda and given a tour. The next day, we met Coach Jackson, his staff, and most of the players. It was tremendous. Remember, I'd dreamed of someday being a Raider. So this was, almost literally, a dream come true.

Yeah, I met Darren McFadden and Rolando Mc-Clain. I actually wear McClain's jersey on Sundays. I like his game. I got to know Shane Lechler a little bit. That was an honor. He's only one of the best punters in NFL history and holds numerous team records—all the more impressive when you consider that Hall of Famer Ray Guy punted for the Silver and Black in the '70s and '80s. Richard Seymour was a very cool dude. But the guy I bonded with was Marcel Reece, the starting fullback. Dude averages, like, one carry a game: His job is to clear holes and pick up blitzes and sacrifice his body for the team. He reminded me of a wrestler.

My butterflies were bigger than usual before that speech as well. But as soon as I started talking, it was like the start of a wrestling match—you forget your nerves and concentrate on the process. I shared my story and related to them that we all have challenges. Rather than being overwhelmed by them, I urged the guys to look forward, to focus on the next step, to avoid dwelling on the past, to be unstoppable.

It went over well. "I got to meet Anthony Robles,"

said strong safety Tyvon Branch via Twitter, "he's outstanding inspired me so much what a guy! And he's a
lifelong raider fan!"

"Just met [Anthony Robles] and his family. . . .
Huge inspiration to all athletes and fans. . . . great fam,"
tweeted Reece.

Before the Bears game the next day, we got sideline
passes during warm-ups. I got to stand right next to the
team during the opening kickoff. What an incredible
adrenaline rush that was. And then during a TV timeout, I was escorted onto the field. While the announcer
talked about my NCAA title, footage from the final
match flashed up on the Jumbotron. When the camera
lingered on my Raiders tattoo, the crowd went crazy.

A lot of times if I don't have a speaking engagement I'll
head over to ASU wrestling practice and help out as an
assistant. Other days, I'll practice jiujitsu. Once I'm a
little more comfortable with that, I might take up boxing. As it happens, wrestling, jiujitsu, and boxing make
up the three elements of Mixed Martial Arts. And what
I hear is that wrestling is the most valuable background
to have for MMA. Because it means you're better able
to stop takedowns, to take people down; and since you're
good on the mat, you can grapple and then unleash
what's known as the "ground and pound" attack, à la

Cain Velasquez, the one-time Ultimate Fighting Championship heavyweight title holder and two-time all-American wrestler at Arizona State.

You see where this is going.

In December, I flew to L.A. to make an appearance on a TV show called *Inside MMA*, where the hosts asked me, of course, if I would consider crossing over to their sport, as so many college wrestlers had before me. ASU alone has put four of its former grapplers in the UFC. As one of the viewers pointed out via Twitter, the UFC has plans to bring in a brand-new weight class: 125 pounds. Judy is vehemently opposed to the idea of me going into the cage: She doesn't want me to get hit in the face. I don't want to get hit in the face, either, but there are days—forgive me, Lord—where I wouldn't mind hitting someone else in the face.

There's this poignant custom in wrestling. Upon completion of his final match, a wrestler will sometimes remove his shoes and leave them in the center of the mat. The great superheavyweight Rulon Gardner did it at the Athens Olympics after earning a bronze medal.

"To leave them on the mat meant I left everything on the mat as a wrestler," he said.

It's a symbolic way of honoring the sport, of saying that you put everything you had into it, down to your shoes. It's also a wrestler's way of saying, uncategorically, I'm done.

I didn't leave my shoes on the mat in Philly in March 2011. I'm not saying I'm not done. I'm just saying that I'm leaving my options open.

I was deeply honored to learn that the National Wrestling Hall of Fame would be presenting me, the following June, with the Medal of Courage, "given to a wrestler who has overcome insurmountable challenges." Insurmountable means, literally, not surmountable, and I don't know that I've ever been faced with a problem that I consider insurmountable. But I know what they mean and, again, I am humbled by the honor.

Gary told me that the Hall of Fame has asked for the purple-and-gold singlet from my days as a Jackrabbit, to put in the exhibit dedicated to me. I didn't want to seem like an ingrate, but I couldn't bring myself to hand it over. That singlet is more than an article of clothing. It's like my armor, my shield. I mean, I bled in it, sweated in it, cried in it. It's as if it's a part of me, almost. Whenever I look at it, it's a source of pride for me. It's like my banner, my flag. There's no way I can give it up. Maybe the high school can find a singlet the same size, and I'll give that to the Hall of Fame.

There are times when I'm itching to get back in the fray, and there are times when I wonder why I would ever want to do that if I didn't *have* to. I love what I'm doing now, bringing my message of hope to people, teaching them to become unstoppable.

UNSTOPPABLE

ON Valentine's Day 2012, I traveled to Marine Corps Base Camp Pendleton, an hour north of San Diego. More than three hundred Marines, wounded in combat and noncombat, would be competing to make an elite team of fifty to represent the Corps at the annual Warrior Games in Colorado Springs. The three hundred Marines I mingled and competed with were members of the Wounded Warrior Regiment. Many had left limbs in Afghanistan or Iraq, the result of gunshot wounds or improvised explosive devices. I've never seen so many amputees in one place. I've never seen so many multiple amputees.

I was with my people!

The first day, I ended up playing wheelchair basketball for hours. Because of my upper body strength, I was fast, even though I wasn't used to my chair. I kept up and was able to play good defense. My shooting was terrible. In archery, I was all over the place at first. But once I settled down and started to lock in, I got hot. I know I got at least one bull's-eye.

One of the more accurate archers I saw was a one-armed Marine whose bowstring had a tab that he pulled back with his teeth. It was adaptive, it was resourceful—very much the Marine way of operating. Everyone had problems, but no one was looking for excuses. They were all about finding a way to get the job done.

What impressed me most was the way they carried themselves. I've had twenty-three-plus years to adjust to my situation. The soldiers I met had been injured only two or three years—or two or three months—ago. It was just so deeply inspiring to see how they were adapting and thriving. It was also impossible not to notice the strong bonds between them; their mutual, collective sense of belonging to this huge family.

I was the featured speaker at the banquet that night, under a vast tent near the WWR's barracks. After I was introduced, the Marines gave me a standing ovation. There I was, looking out at these beautiful warriors who had sacrificed body parts for a cause greater than themselves. Many stood despite lacking one or both legs. Many applauded, whether they had two hands or not. For the first time in my brief career as a speaker, I had difficulty starting my speech.

Once I mastered control of my emotions and got rolling, I was fine. I remember looking up during that speech, after telling the story of how I wasn't recruited out of high school, despite having won a national championship. I saw Marines nodding; they could relate to that experience. They knew how it felt to be seen as incomplete, not as good as everybody else, because they were different. It's the never-ending, uphill battle that we fight.

I was there for a couple of days and talked to them about a lot of things. I was surprised, and a little sad, to find out how maxed out a lot of them felt at the strain placed on them and their families by multiple deployments. As far as our missing limbs went, I didn't ask what happened to them, and they didn't ask what happened to me. We didn't really care. The fact of the matter is it happened, and everyone was moving forward.

When I got back to the airport in Phoenix, I called Gary. I was still in awe of the experience. "That was the best event I've done so far," I told him. "If I was not a motivational speaker, I would be a Marine."

He surprised me with his reply:

"But, son, they wouldn't let you join." I think he was just trying to push my buttons.

"Why not?" I replied. "I can do everything they can do."

I was smiling, walking through the parking structure on the way to my truck, thinking the same thought that crosses my mind whenever someone tells me there's something I can't do:

Try stopping me.

ACKNOWLEDGMENTS

THIS book would not have been possible without my cowriter, Austin Murphy. It wasn't easy finding someone I could develop a bond and chemistry with, but Austin and I hit it off immediately. His three decades of experience at *Sports Illustrated* really helped. We had a lot of interviews over the course of many months, and I walked away from each session excited for the next one.

I'll tell you straight up: I've never been one to go deep, to really talk about my feelings with others. It wasn't difficult reliving the great moments, like when I won my wrestling titles. But this project forced me to dissect and analyze and confront certain painful, uncomfortable memories that I would have otherwise left alone. In a way, working on this book was therapeutic for me.

I'm so fortunate to have Gary Lewis as my manager. He's instrumental in the release of this book, helping me sign as a Nike athlete as well as my signing with the Washington Speakers Bureau. He feels more like a family member than a business partner, and I truly believe that there was some grand plan for our paths to cross. Gary is one of the people who I have been blessed to have in my life as someone who I can respect and learn from. His character is second to none. I see Gary as both a father figure and friend, and I love him as such.

Thanks also to Travers Johnson and Gotham Books/ Penguin for taking my life story and putting it out there for thousands to read. I can remember flying out to New York City for our first meeting with Gotham. We walked into that meeting not sure what exactly to expect. But by the end of it, we didn't want to leave. The Gotham/ Penguin people are not only friendly but really good at what they do: I'm blessed to have such a great team, and I'd like to give a special thanks to Lindsay Gordon, William Shinker, Lisa Johnson, Laura Gianino, Jessica Chun, Dick Heffernan, LeeAnn Pemberton, and all the others who played a role in bringing this book together.

Major league thanks also to "The Big Unit" Randy Johnson (!!!!) for shooting the photograph for my book cover. It was an honor getting to work with him. Throughout the book, I talk about some of the people I was blessed

Acknowledgments

to have in my life and who really helped me become Unstoppable. Some of the great friends who deserve recognition:

- I would have never started wrestling if it hadn't been for my cousin Jesse Ochoa, who introduced me to the sport and saw potential in me from the very beginning.

- Special thanks goes to Arizona State assistant wrestling coach Brian Stith, who happens to be one of my best friends and played a huge roll in helping me bounce back after my junior-year loss at Nationals. Before he became a coach, we wrestled for a year on the same team. Those bonds are strong: Whenever I felt like I needed extra help with my wrestling, Brian went above and beyond the call, whether it was staying after practice, helping me review previous matches, or sending me scouting reports on the next wrestler that we needed to take out. Sometimes I just needed someone to goof off with, to forget about the pressure. Stith was excellent at that, too. We're video game buddies; *Battlefield* is our game of choice—any gamers out there, you're welcome to mix it up with us. But be warned: We can get pretty intense.

- I could not have won my title without my training partners Orlando Jimenez, Carlos Castro, and Dalton Miller. Those guys pushed me hard during every practice at ASU.

- Thank you to Joel and Judy Weldon, who have helped me tremendously in mentoring me on what it takes to be an inspirational speaker. Joel Weldon was my speaking coach. He worked with me and came up with the theme of being Unstoppable.

- My high school assistant coach Dave Di-Domenico. It was awesome getting to wrestle for Coach D. He expected three things out of each and every one of his wrestlers, and he would preach them regularly: show up, work hard, and be coachable. If you did these things, Coach D. was the best to be around, and I loved the guy.

- Thank you to Travis Koppenhafer for helping me fine-tune my tilts in college, and to Chris Drouin, Ray and Connie Fikes, Dan Sager, Frank Popolizio, Arnold

Acknowledgments

Alpert, Henry Cejudo, Aaron Simpson, Ryan Bader, C. B. Dolloway, Cain Velasquez, and Cliff Keen wrestling gear. Thank you to John Vassallo, Tim Johnson, and ESPN for welcoming me into their family as a commentator and for their huge hand in helping to promote my book. Also, I am incredibly honored to call myself a Nike athlete. So thank you, Nike, for all the support.

I would also like to thank my dad, Ron. Even though our relationship has been strained over the years, I love him and he is my dad. So it was difficult to write about those bad times. Talking with family and friends, however, it became clear to me that I needed to tell my whole story to help give hope to those who might be facing similar challenges. My dad has taught me a lot in my life; there have been plenty of good things I learned from him that have made me the man I am—things that one day I will pass on to my kids. Unfortunately there were also some things that I've told myself I will never do. That's life, I guess. With success comes some failure.

I'm sure there are plenty of people who make up what I like to call Team Unstoppable who I am forgetting to thank, but they know who they are, and they know I'm grateful. Finally, I want to thank the sport of wrestling, which is so close to my heart and has forever changed my life. It's more than just a sport, and I'm honored to be a part of the wrestling community. It was Dan Gable who said, "Once you've wrestled, everything else in life is easy." And it's true.